Daddy Roy Matlock's
You Cannots

Volume I
Common Sense, Education, Faith and Values

by

Roy L Matlock, Sr.

WESTVIEW BOOK PUBLISHING, INC
Nashville, Tennessee

ISBN 1-933912-54-5

Printed in the United States of America on acid-free paper

First Edition, May 2007

Cover design by Hugh Daniel and Roy L. Matlock, Sr.

Edited by Bob Allen, Judy Allen, and Clementine Barfield, Author's Corner, LLC

Author Representative: Bob Allen, Author's Corner, LLC

WESTVIEW BOOK PUBLISHING, INC.
P.O. Box 210183
Nashville, Tennessee 37221
www.westviewpublishing.com

This book is dedicated to my wife, Martha, for her support and encouragement to publish the more than four thousand *You Cannots* that I have generated over the years.

I also want to dedicate this book to my five children – Linda, Judy, Mickie, Roy Jr., and William who have personally endured my telling them these *You Cannots,* and as you will notice are obviously the source from which many of these one-line witticisms are derived.

In addition, I would like to dedicate these *You Cannots* to all students.

Foreword

For several decades, Daddy Roy L. Matlock, Sr. has generated common horse sense, educational, factual, fun and entertaining 'witicisms' and 'one-liners' beginning with "*You cannot* …" His more than four thousand *You Cannots* are now presented in two volumes titled *Daddy Roy Matlock's You Cannots – Common Sense, Education, Faith and Values* and *Daddy Roy Matlock's You Cannots – Business, Finance, Government, Taxes and More Common Sense.*

As you read these *You Cannots*, you will recall your own life's experiences and chuckle how the author expresses his common sense view of raising his family, managing his business, maintaining a strong faith, and life in general.

Daddy Roy Matlock's
You Cannots

Volume I
Common Sense, Education, Faith, and Values

You cannot fail to get more knowledge by reading this book.

You cannot have but one way to go when you are famous, and that is infamous.

You cannot have but one way to go when you are famous, and that is infamous.

You cannot stop church from being a hospital for sinners.

You cannot stop Satan from constantly trying to tempt you.

You cannot find people who think they know it all after they find out what all really is.

You cannot stop race car drivers from spinning their wheels.

You cannot catch lightning in a bottle.

You cannot have a good mind if you don't use it well.

You cannot prevent some people from needing brain food.

You cannot starve doubt unless you feed it faith.

You cannot keep going in the wrong direction if you want to keep going; God allows U turns.

You cannot stop success from being more attitude than aptitude.

You cannot stop friends from coming and going, but enemies seem to accumulate.

You cannot stop some of your friends from walking in when others walk out.

You cannot find people that have seen a rat race.

You cannot prevent attitude from being just as important as gratitude.

You cannot stop procrastination from stealing your time.

You cannot find but one thing you can give and still keep; that is your word.

You cannot stop actions from speaking louder than words, but they do not do it more often.

You cannot stop success from coming in *'can'* while failure comes in *'can'ts'*.

You cannot stop experience from being what men call "correcting their mistakes."

You cannot stop some people from waking up and finding out they are a success and have not been asleep.

You cannot be too careful on your way up of how you treat people because you may run into them on your way down.

You cannot find anyone more qualified to be you than yourself.

You cannot always be right, but there is no shame in correcting your mistakes.

You cannot prevent ambition from being like hunger ... it obeys no law but its appetite.

You cannot find many people who have no vices, except the ones who have very annoying virtues.

You cannot stop some good things from coming, out of dreaming.

You cannot stop smart men from changing their mind or making changes for improvement.

You cannot prevent the road to success from always being under construction.

You cannot find any bird that can fly in any direction; up, down, left, right, forward and backwards except a hummingbird.

You cannot break a bad habit unless you drop it.

You cannot cheer yourself up easier than to cheer someone else up.

You cannot get rid of fear by not applying faith.

You cannot get happiness to choose you; you have to choose it.

You cannot fail to prepare unless you want to fail.

You cannot get a calm sea to make a good sailor.

You cannot find but one person who was perfect; and they killed Him.

You cannot lie louder than when you are lying to yourself.

You cannot have any greater fault than to think you do not have any.

You cannot find a right way to do something wrong to someone.

You cannot be correct as easy as you can be critical.

You cannot find an easier way to end a quarrel than forgiving.

You cannot be too careful with a sharp tongue; you may even cut your own throat.

You cannot prevent it from taking more muscles to frown than to smile.

You cannot weave anything more important than your expression.

You cannot stop the deaf and the blind from hearing and seeing kindness.

You cannot carry a load heavier than a grudge.

You cannot stop a load you are carrying from breaking you down unless you change the way you are carrying it.

You cannot be wrong nearly as many times if you will think twice before you speak once.

You cannot prevent tact from being able to see the way people want you to see them, but not like what they really are.

You cannot always be on the road to success; there may be a few potholes in the road.

You cannot prevent diplomacy from being able to let some one else win to get your point across.

You cannot have very good thoughts if you are unhappy with the way your life is going.

You cannot cry over spilled milk nearly as long if it is condensed.

You cannot prevent one good deed from being a lot better than a lot of good intentions.

You cannot stop brushing the teeth you want to keep.

You cannot stop using your brain if you want to be educated.

You cannot just do it enough to be average unless you want to stay average.

You cannot succeed unless you try.

You cannot stop some people from driving like they own the road instead of the car.

You cannot stop riding a horse in the direction it is going.

You cannot stop itches from always being where you don't want people to see where you are scratching.

You cannot have a place in the sun unless you are willing to put up with a few blisters.

You cannot stop worrying from being about something before it happens.

You cannot get as many people to work as you can to worry.

You cannot get some trouble from starting out as fun.

You cannot prevent what you know from counting, but it is also important of what you think of in time.

You cannot be concerned about which road you are on if you don't know where you are going because any road will get you there.

You cannot stop some people from hiring some people smarter than they are to help them look smart.

You cannot fail to put your goals in writing and looking at them often if you intend to reach them.

You cannot stop doing what you believe in and love.

You cannot prevent getting run over even if you are on the right track ... unless you move.

You cannot prevent a stopped clock from being right twice a day.

You cannot be like postage stamps unless you want to stay with one thing until you get there.

You cannot stop anger from being just one letter short of danger.

You cannot find a better vitamin to make a friend than B1.

You cannot prevent doing a good job from giving you the opportunity to do more.

You cannot stop being rich if you are happy with what you have.

You cannot have your interest in anything better than your future, because that is where you are going to spend the rest of your life.

You cannot have much tact unless you try to rub out other people's mistakes.

You cannot get men to give away anything more freely than advice.

You cannot stop being positive from being better than being negative.

You cannot stop kindness being spent on some people that don't deserve it.

You cannot recognize most opportunities because they are disguised as hard work.

You cannot find harder work than thinking; that is why so many people don't do it.

You cannot be denied success if you are a go-getter.

You cannot get golf balls to listen when you talk to them; they turn off their hearing aids.

You cannot blame all of your shortcomings on somebody else.

You cannot go by the rules if somebody keeps changing them.

You cannot tell one lie and not expect to have to tell more lies to cover up the first one.

You cannot stop welfare as long as you do not require work to eat.

You cannot live the life of the rich and famous by not working.

You cannot have a complete family life when you do not contribute.

You cannot have freedom without knowledge.

You cannot build character and be a liar.

You cannot be successful unless you prepare yourself for success.

You cannot fall for anything if you stand for something.

You cannot have power without knowledge

You cannot use people and discard them like paper cups and not eventually be discarded.

You cannot hide being a con artist indefinitely.

You cannot be a con artist and escape being conned.

You cannot be two-faced and be labeled as being credible.

You cannot have any better than just the right amount of everything.

You cannot keep up unless you read.

You cannot depend on social security for retirement.

You cannot change the scenery unless you are the lead dog.

You cannot be a leader if you do not take the lead.

You cannot be a leader if you can never find anything wrong to make right.

You cannot have character and character flaws at the same time.

You cannot improve your character unless you correct your flaws.

You cannot be educated unless you continue to read.

You cannot live above your means and retire in your normal lifestyle.

You cannot help yourself or anyone else by keeping all of your knowledge inside; you must impart it to others.

You cannot be a good loser and be a winner.

You cannot prevent suckers from being born every minute.

You cannot tell lies and be trusted at the same time.

You cannot satisfy people's greed of thinking they can't get something for nothing.

You cannot prevent the suckers from thinking they can get something for nothing.

You cannot lie and expect to not have to tell more lies to try to get out of the first lie.

You cannot build character telling lies.

You cannot ignore people that need help and not need help at sometime or another.

You cannot be educated unless you participate in continuing education.

You cannot expect true feelings for yourself unless you have true feeling for others.

You cannot believe that waste is better than conserving and not come out on the short end of the stick.

You cannot expect respect if you don't show respect for others.

You cannot strengthen the poor and weak by weakening the strong and healthy.

You cannot further equality by inciting class hatred.

You cannot build quality character and courage by taking away a man's will, initiative and independence.

You cannot help men forever by doing for them what they can and should do for themselves.

You cannot lie to the person in the mirror.

You cannot ignore crime and expect it to go away.

You cannot make promises you know you cannot keep and expect to be trusted.

You cannot be slick and not be caught ... even as slick as chitterlings and snails are, they get eaten.

You cannot throw stuff on the wall and not expect it to fall off.

You cannot expect to get rid of waste when you are the creator of waste.

You cannot hire somebody to worry for you.

You cannot have a healthy brain unless you exercise it.

You cannot be educated unless you continue to educate yourself.

You cannot get enough knowledge unless you read enough.

You cannot know when you get there if you don't know where you are going.

You cannot be a winner if all you think about is losing.

You cannot correct anything that is wrong if you just look for what is right.

You cannot make things better unless you are able to detect what is wrong.

You cannot expect to need more than five fingers when you count your true friends.

You cannot be a rooster and produce eggs without a hen.

You cannot keep your teeth if you ignore them.

You cannot play all your life unless you love your work.

You cannot conveniently forget to give messages and non-credible excuses for not doing something and expect to be received as being a credible person.

You cannot jump big puddles unless you are willing to take big strides.

You cannot be nicknamed 'Slick Willie' and be trusted.

You cannot cheat when you play a game and not eventually get caught.

You cannot play solitaire and cheat and not know who gets cheated.

You cannot see the future by looking in the rear view mirror.

You cannot complete this book because you can keep adding your own *You Cannots*.

You cannot be required to serve time behind bars for singing to loud in the church choir.

You cannot hit unless you shoot.

You cannot have much more trouble reading a map than you can have folding it.

You cannot have a conference with less than two people.

You cannot prevent applied knowledge from being good and bad.

You cannot get women to be equal to men unless you teach them to be as lazy as men.

You cannot laugh at your own mistakes and condemn others for making the same mistakes.

You cannot stop cowards from dying a thousand times, but a brave man dies only once.

You cannot have respect for the truth unless you tell it.

11

You cannot sometimes talk about your pain unless you are talking about your husband, wife, boss, girlfriend, boyfriend, family or friends.

You cannot complain about thorns if you want roses.

You cannot fry your brain with drugs and expect it to keep you out of trouble.

You cannot smoke cigarettes or marijuana and also live a long time.

You cannot get Satan to teach you to do what's right.

You cannot heal emotional wounds better or faster than with laughter.

You cannot stop all seeing and hearing.

You cannot have too much honesty.

You cannot have anything new if it has just been used once.

You cannot make this life last forever, but you can the next one.

You cannot act like Lucifer and teach your children to do what's right.

You cannot have to remember what you said if you tell the truth.

You cannot have world peace until you solve world food problems.

You cannot find as many opportunities as you can make.

You cannot prevent minds from being parachutes; they work better when they are open.

You cannot prevent people who are at the top from finding ways to get to the bottom.

You cannot find more skilled repairmen or repairwomen than doctors.

You cannot conceal ignorance with anything except knowledge.

You cannot stop intelligence from creating wealth and a better lifestyle.

You cannot stop intelligent people from finding ways to make things more efficient.

You cannot find anything that has more extremes than right and wrong.

You cannot take the advantage of opportunity when it knocks unless you open the door and invite it to stay for dinner.

You cannot see the end from the beginning.

You cannot be independent by yourself alone.

You cannot hear the same type of talk in church that you hear on the golf course.

You cannot work if you do not rest.

You cannot find a greater engineer than God; He designed and built everything and there will never be another.

You cannot stop teaching and training your competitors, but don't teach them everything.

You cannot prevent intelligence from being a powerful weapon.

You cannot stop intelligent people from being in charge.

You cannot find an easier way to communicate with God than knee mail.

You cannot make more time in a day: there are 24 hours; 1,440 minutes; and 8,640 seconds.

You cannot prevent knowledge from creating wisdom.

You cannot tell when you are going to die.

You cannot be a successful failure.

You cannot save or make time.

You cannot destroy evil except to take away the fertile soil it thrives on.

You cannot find terrorists that have the power to destroy the faith we have in God or the power to destroy the sun, moon, water, oceans, heavens, and earth.

You cannot stop the proper application of knowledge from bringing wisdom and good results.

You cannot prevent your Mom from making you face the music when you try to duck practicing.

You cannot be very popular if you are always looking for fault, but you can if you find remedies.

You cannot stop some people from using religion for good or evil.

You cannot stop some people from getting in the way of other people's progress.

You cannot stop hard work from increasing your luck.

You cannot prevent how much and how hard you search from revealing how much value you place on what you are searching for.

You cannot always tell if you are having a problem or an opportunity.

You cannot stop some people from going where the path leads them, but some people go where there is no path and leave a trail.

You cannot stop what we repeatedly do right from becoming a habit of excellence.

You cannot prevent your thoughts from determining where you are today or where you will be in the future.

You cannot stop doing from being remembered much longer than hearing or seeing.

You cannot prevent a perfect storm from converging into a perfect disaster.

You cannot stop performers from living in houses just as big as they can pay for.

You cannot play it safe unless you stop playing.

You cannot get wood to perform woodworking.

You cannot put your lost mind on a back up disk.

You cannot stop well done from being better than well said.

You cannot stop wisdom from coming with age, but you don't have to tell anyone that is the way you got it.

You cannot recycle time.

You cannot stop people from delaying but time will not.

You cannot stop cheap talk from exceeding demand.

You cannot buy a lasting peace or happiness from the devil.

You cannot evade responsibility today and be happy with what tomorrow brings.

You cannot find a more powerful weapon than the human mouth.

You cannot stop rust from rusting.

You cannot make yourself into a big shot unless you keep on making little shots.

You cannot be required to have a lot of skills and abilities to fire someone; you only have to have the authority.

You cannot have job security when you arrive late, leave early and only do as little as you can get by with.

You cannot have a more costly adjustment than non-adjustment.

You cannot stop some people from being arrogant and sarcastic and not even know it.

You cannot stop some people from thinking preachers are hired guns, but if they are, they have the greatest employer that has ever been.

You cannot have a greater weakness than not knowing you have a weakness.

You cannot get some of your children to understand that you are trying to help them; you are telling them things they should do to protect their own safety even if you tell them the same thing three or four times, in fact, it might make them mad.

You cannot get some people to realize that the junk they are saving will not be the treasures for others so they just keep saving junk.

You cannot stop strong willed people from having disagreements with others.

You cannot prevent some children from departing from what they were taught when they were young even though they were taught right.

You cannot have spectacular results unless you make a lot of unspectacular preparations.

You cannot practice too much if you want to excel in what you are practicing for.

You cannot blame other people for not doing what you know you should do without being told.

You cannot read these *You Cannots* and not learn some ways that you could improve yourself.

You cannot wait until your children are grown to teach them what you should have taught them when they were children.

You cannot stop intelligent people from finding a better way.

You cannot find many people who can steer a ship during a storm.

You cannot stop some people from needing to adjust, but most of them don't know it.

You cannot stop some things from causing you to lose your eternal life.

You cannot find many people that will accept the responsibility or the results of doing what they did even if they knew it was wrong before they did it.

You cannot pay too much for education, but if you pay too little the price of ignorance becomes very expensive.

You cannot prevent some people from creating opportunities for others with their money.

You cannot stop people from wanting more things or stuff.

You cannot stop people from doing what they like best.

You cannot stop some people from having bad habits and improving on them.

You cannot stop parents from creating followers and leaders, even if they are teaching them to do what is right.

You cannot stop habits from being good and bad.

You cannot be the first one to ever be hated or persecuted.

You cannot blame others for not doing what you should have done or should not have done and not be considered a buck passer.

You cannot be very happy when you have to eat crow.

You cannot put a price on good manners.

You cannot wait to dig a well until you are thirsty; it is too late.

You cannot get most people to realize there is a safety hazard that exists until after they should have corrected the problem and even after this time they try to blame the accident as someone else's fault.

You cannot always prevent how you say something from being more important than what you say.

You cannot have a finish line if you want to be a real winner.

You cannot have anything more essential to education than character; it is the basis of right and wrong.

You cannot stop some people's hair from backing up.

You cannot leave this world with anything.

You cannot know how much is enough.

You cannot find un-level ground at the foot of the cross.

You cannot say *"why didn't I think of that first"* if you did.

You cannot hang on to status quo if you want things to change; you have to change.

You cannot be too busy to say thanks unless you want to get fewer opportunities to do so.

You cannot wear your body out by doing nothing; it will happen automatically.

You cannot do just as little as you are expected to do and thrive, but do less and you may not survive.

You cannot quit trying if you lose unless you want to lose.

You cannot really be in the groove if you are in a rut.

You cannot fail to adapt and hem and haw; change is part of life.

You cannot stop people from doing something they really don't want to, but the ones that don't find an excuse.

You cannot stop some people from still believing in themselves, even if most everyone else stops.

You cannot prevent attitude from being just as important as aptitude.

You cannot prevent a three-inch tongue from killing a six-foot man.

You cannot scatter a pillow full of feathers to the wind and ever find all of them.

You cannot know how well you have been blessed if you are a '*can do*' person instead of one that always finds excuses of why you can't.

You cannot stop caskets from asking other caskets if they are coffin.

You cannot climb higher than the ladder you select.

You cannot have a gift of happiness unless you unwrap it.

You cannot stop ignorance from being more expensive than education.

You cannot have the perfect grass even if it is on the other side of the street; it will still have to be mowed.

You cannot get rid of an enemy any better than making a friend out of them.

You cannot prevent some people from using stumbling blocks for stepping stones.

You cannot stop some lecturers from sounding like they are talking in their sleep.

You cannot prevent people that go on diets from running into snacks.

You cannot stop goals from having dead lines.

You cannot stop a man that wants to do something from finding a way to get it done; but a man who doesn't will find an excuse.

You cannot change many minds with anger.

You cannot get caught up if you quit while you are behind.

You cannot stop Christmas from bringing jingle bills.

You cannot go to heaven if you don't stop raising hell here on earth and accept the Man upstairs as your savior.

You cannot prevent eyes from believing themselves and ears from believing others.

You cannot have a cat scan of your soul, but this does not mean that it does not exist.

You cannot stay awake to enjoy a good night's sleep.

You cannot stop some people from looking the way they feel ... good or bad.

You cannot get up in the morning if you don't go to bed at night.

You cannot prevent some people from getting up in the morning and putting on a fresh grouch.

You cannot step on someone else's toe if you put your own foot in your mouth.

You cannot stop two letters in the alphabet from being an important function in your life ... I and C.

You cannot stop some people from having a closed mind when their mouth is open.

You cannot stop baseball players from spitting on a regular basis; they don't even realize they are doing it.

You cannot prevent it from showing if you are uninformed.

You cannot really find people that sweat blood, but they may think they are.

You cannot be a happy pessimist by looking at the success of others.

You cannot have any more individuality than your fingerprints.

You cannot always leave happier when you leave some people or places.

You cannot prevent great men from showing their greatness by the way they treat little men that are not so great.

You cannot stop some people from hanging on when they get to the end of their rope; they tie a knot and hang on.

You cannot leave home without your fingerprints.

You cannot prevent a wordless prayer from being a real prayer.

You cannot realize the extent of your ignorance without having a considerable amount of knowledge.

You cannot stop some people from being like 10-speed bicycles; they both have gears that are never used.

You cannot bite the hand that feeds you unless you want to stop eating.

You cannot find a bigger room than the room for improvement.

You cannot prevent some people from showing that they lack a vocabulary to express themselves by the language they use.

You cannot stop missing some golf shots if your golf grips are slick.

You cannot sail without air, *You cannot* make more air, and *You cannot* make air non-essential.

You cannot be perfect, but you can be forgiven.

You cannot stop doors from sometimes being *'a jar'*.

You cannot stop sharing the air we breathe.

You cannot prevent each experience from being a learning experience.

You cannot prevent the naked truth from being better than the best-dressed lies.

You cannot prevent good fences from making better neighbors.

You cannot be a good teacher unless you teach your students how to get along without your help.

You cannot get out of trouble nearly as easy as you can get in.

You cannot keep friendships as easy as you can make them.

You cannot prevent good humor from being one of the best articles of dress one can wear.

You cannot stop some people from taking life-threatening risks.

You cannot necessarily believe anything I say; I did not inhale or cut down a cherry tree either.

You cannot thread a needle unless you have an eye for it.

You cannot do it if you cannot dream it.

You cannot have but one savior to save you from hell.

You cannot find many drivers that speed when they can see a police car in the rear view mirror.

You cannot stop knowledge from being power so why not get all you can.

You cannot follow the devil and have everlasting life.

You cannot make fishing as enjoyable as catching.

You cannot stop it from being risky to not take a risk.

You cannot be as concerned when your children are not listening to you as you should be when they are watching you.

You cannot be or keep on being educated unless you keep on educating yourself by your own actions.

You cannot forget and smile if you continue to remember and be sad.

You cannot make how long you live as important as you can make how you live.

You cannot stop men from dying, but their deeds live on.

You cannot prevent the mirror from reflecting the image of what is in front of it.

You cannot test the depth of a deep river with both feet.

You cannot really have success unless you prepare yourself to take advantage of your success.

You cannot fail to read and be any more knowledgeable than the person that cannot read.

You cannot limit the freedom of others and not limit your own.

You cannot stop cowards from dying many deaths, but the brave man experiences death only once.

You cannot explain why we park on driveways and drive on parkways.

You cannot prevent some people from sowing the seeds while others only receive the harvest.

You cannot believe that all people that marry continue to believe they married the right person the first time.

You cannot have a soft pillow unless you have a clear conscience.

You cannot have a better punishment when one of your children does wrong than asking the child to punish you for not teaching the child to not do what is wrong.

You cannot be immune from ignorance unless you have knowledge.

You cannot prevent a lot of men from liking their wife's mother-in-law better than they do their own.

You cannot be sure that you will not find out that lettuce is not fattening after all.

You cannot prevent good judgment from coming from experience and good experience coming from bad experiences.

You cannot cut down your risk by not taking any.

You cannot pay a lower price for freedom than allowing others to be free.

You cannot find a cure for the common birthday.

You cannot read bad books and be any better off than the person who can't read.

You cannot raise your have level until you raise your want level.

You cannot spread your bread on the water and expect it to come back toasted.

You cannot find an over supply of moral courage.

You cannot find people that learn everything in school.

You cannot lose anything by discarding your faults.

You cannot stop adults from being obsolete children.

You cannot have a worse disability than having a bad attitude.

You cannot ever get men and women to agree if the toilet seat should be left up or down.

You cannot get a pessimist to agree that the glass is half full instead of half empty.

You cannot always be different, best, or first.

You cannot share a secret.

You cannot condemn the mirror for what it reflects.

You cannot find the road to life too steep if you just do what's right.

You cannot remain on the right track unless you change tracks to keep from getting run over.

You cannot find anything much more brilliant than a lightning bug, but it still does not have a mind.

You cannot change men very easily except when they are babies.

You cannot find a more predictable way to predict the future unless you understand the present.

You cannot have to take your own medicine if you keep your mouth shut.

You cannot stay young mentally unless you stop learning.

You cannot stop success from being the product of education.

You cannot give yourself permission to succeed unless you educate yourself.

You cannot have a resurrection until there has been a death.

You cannot realize the value of education if you don't have it.

You cannot stop believing that two heads are better than one, especially when they are kissing.

You cannot prevent New Years' resolutions from conflicting with old habits.

You cannot stop a bucket from getting full even if you fill it with a thimble.

You cannot make a dog understand the difference between a new shoe and an old shoe.

You cannot stop the wind from blowing or the sun from shining.

You cannot destroy water.

You cannot stop the snow and rain from falling.

You cannot get history to repeat itself, but fools repeat history.

You cannot swim half way across the river and not drown; you must swim the other half.

You cannot be blessed any more than have two ears to listen and only one mouth to talk because you learn a lot more listening than you do talking.

You cannot stop youth from being wasted on the young.

You cannot do just enough to get by if you want to climb the ladder of success.

You cannot have a train of thought if you have no terminal or track to run them on.

You cannot stop the early bird from getting the worms no more than you can stop the second mouse from getting the cheese.

You cannot stop some graduates from appearing to receive master degrees in ignorance.

You cannot always go by the majority; if the majority were right, the majority would be rich.

You cannot find turtles on top of fence posts that did not have some help getting there.

You cannot prevent silence from being consent.

You cannot get meowing cats to catch mice.

You cannot sleep with dogs and not get fleas.

You cannot find people that have enough knowledge to take away your knowledge.

You cannot really want the good old days unless you want to turn off the air conditioning, television, and go to the toilet in the back yard.

You cannot stop opinions from being like armpits; everyone is entitled to them.

You cannot know what to do, when you do not know what to do until you get the wisdom to know what to do.

You cannot stop good ideas from coming up in the middle of the night.

You cannot be happy if you are on the right track if you are going in the wrong direction.

You cannot stop people from misusing knowledge.

You cannot stand any taller than when you stoop down to help a child in need.

You cannot determine the character of a man until you know the size of the things that make him bad.

You cannot become better if you continue to be bitter.

You cannot stop some people from complaining about getting a little mud when they are praying for rain.

You cannot sit if you are babysitting and especially if the babies are triplets or if the baby is a grandson named Will.

You cannot stop people from trying to profit from your knowledge.

You cannot deliver the goods if your heart is heavier than the load.

You cannot find anything interesting if you are not interested.

You cannot be moral unless you tell the truth.

You cannot not easily sit on a crack that is not your own.

You cannot act and dress like a street person unless you want to be treated like one.

You cannot prevent knowledge from increasing or decreasing fear.

You cannot have good friends who get in the way when you are going down.

You cannot have an over abundance of honesty.

You cannot be on the wrong road if you don't know where you are going.

You cannot level the playing field any better than having a better idea.

You cannot stop some people from seeing where they are going if you bury them face down.

You cannot find anything that has sat its way to success except a hen.

You cannot stop pessimist from looking at the future and only seeing trouble.

You cannot stop people from wanting to be placed in their casket facing the direction of where they want to go.

You cannot have a good education unless you know what to do with it.

You cannot tell how hard or easy marriage can be until you try it.

You cannot have vision unless you can dream.

You cannot transport more valuable cargo than driving a school bus.

You cannot read silence as a yes or no.

You cannot be sure about the weather or love.

You cannot stop people from sending messages with their hearts when they write letters.

You cannot be wise unless you learn what to overlook.

You cannot benefit from a good idea unless you put it to work.

You cannot stop bad things from happening to good people.

You cannot be blessed any better than having two ends; one to think with and the other to sit on.

You cannot find a tougher game than golf.

You cannot find a better place to store dead batteries than in flashlights.

You cannot trust anyone who has no respect for the truth.

You cannot get stale if you keep up with change.

You cannot have security without friends.

You cannot hang your hat on the same nail very long if you are a natural-born rambler.

You cannot stop fog from settling in some people's brains.

You cannot stop the fake finger wag.

You cannot prevent dead people from looking up at tombstones.

You cannot learn very much if you think you already know it all.

You cannot find a better place to go than heaven.

You cannot follow the crowd if you want to be successful.

You cannot stop knowledge from being the road map to success.

You cannot get an agreement between a man and wife of who should be in charge of the remote control.

You cannot stop masonry from making good men better.

You cannot stop who you know from being beneficial to what you know.

You cannot have better revenge than having success.

You cannot maintain a relationship or marriage with beauty alone.

You cannot reach your destination unless you have one.

You cannot stop good things from being evil.

You cannot stop people from going to hell by choice.

You cannot prevent problems from temporarily slowing you down, but only you can stop them from being permanent.

You cannot live off of your community; you must live in it.

You cannot lead if you don't know when to leave.

You cannot have much fun living with misers, but they make great ancestors.

You cannot find anything to change the heart any better than the heart.

You cannot regret the past when you have loving children.

You cannot have to wipe your face nearly as much when you laugh as you do when you cry.

You cannot stop some men and women from committing adultery at least in their heart or mind.

You cannot improve the city unless you live in the country.

You cannot go to heaven except by invitation from God.

You cannot enjoy frugal ancestors any more than when they leave you in their will or trust.

You cannot stop friction unless you apply the oil of kindness.

You cannot prevent symphony when you have two hearts pulling in the same direction.

You cannot appreciate flying unless you land.

You cannot prevent people from failing to say thank you, but the people that don't get fewer and fewer chances to do so.

You cannot believe everything you read in newspapers, but it will keep you informed on what is going on, good or bad.

You cannot really be honest unless you are honest when nobody is looking.

You cannot stop bad habits from being like good beds, easy to get into but hard to get out of.

33

You cannot stop the truth from being like a rubber band; the more you stretch it, the weaker it gets.

You cannot believe that all nice people finish the game last because a lot of them are winners before they ever start the game.

You cannot tickle and amuse yourself; your brain knows what you are up to.

You cannot have a secret when someone tells you to let this be just our little secret; the urge for one of the two to tell or brag about it is just too great.

You cannot lie on the couch when talking to your psychiatrist if you want to get help, you must tell the truth.

You cannot stop young boys and girls from being good to look at so they can be tolerated until they acquire sense.

You cannot find a bigger heater than the sun.

You cannot stop some people from criticizing you even when you are doing what's right.

You cannot stay on a diet as easy as you can buy bigger clothes.

You cannot always blame bad report cards on the student; sometimes it is heredity or lack of parent teaching.

You cannot stop strong willed children from taking advantage of weak parents.

You cannot build your house with cards and not get blown away.

You cannot keep a secret even when you whisper it into your best friend's ear.

You cannot always believe people when they wag their finger and say they did not do something.

You cannot find lace that is not full of holes.

You cannot have enough mature people in the right places.

You cannot stop dancers' performances from resting on their legs.

You cannot stop killing time from killing you.

You cannot ask to be delivered unless you are willing to pay the postage.

You cannot make a path if you follow the trail.

You cannot put a value on hindsight.

You cannot prevent time from passing slow while you are young, but it will speed up as you grow older.

You cannot take your worldly possessions with you when you die.

You cannot dispute the fact that you have two choices of where you will go when you die, and that it is your choice.

You cannot build up what people think of you by wearing sagging pants, tattoos, rings in your nose, eyebrows, tongue rings, and baseball caps turned backwards.

You cannot smile very easily if you keep a stiff upper lip.

You cannot have a more important part of the body than the heart; it controls all the other parts.

You cannot prevent having a long golf game if you choose the wrong foursome.

You cannot get eagles to flock.

You cannot soar with the eagles if you think like a hummingbird.

You cannot make life a science; we make it up as we go.

You cannot stop the silence between the notes that make pretty music.

You cannot stop time from flying even if it does not have wings.

You cannot receive a more valuable pardon than the one you receive at Calvary's tree.

You cannot find anyone that fools and hates as much as Satan, if you follow him you will go where you do not want to go.

You cannot have everything your way.

You cannot be as concerned about what your enemies say about you as you need to be about the silence of your friends.

You cannot prevent television from making lazy people lazier.

You cannot show me a dumb golfer who loses while playing with their boss or customers.

You cannot be forgiven from your sins except by the person who died for us.

You cannot have a better wish than living and dying an honest man or woman.

You cannot have comfortable shoes when you put them on the wrong feet.

You cannot stop life from being a toll road to tomorrow.

You cannot stop fools from rushing in where angels fear to tread.

You cannot get a push if you are not willing to budge.

You cannot build a good reputation on what you intend to do tomorrow; it's what you have done in the past.

You cannot always please all people by doing right, however you will astonish others.

You cannot stop discipline from being unpleasant at the time, but it will make you better off later on.

You cannot tell when a piece of junk will turn out to be an antique.

You cannot mature gracefully unless you learn to accept change.

You cannot be learned unless you learn how to think.

You cannot prevent some people from thinking you are a fool.

You cannot go very far wrong if you follow a good mentor.

You cannot be careless and be safe; carelessness will bite you.

You cannot stop people from believing lies if they think they will benefit and have no interest in truth.

You cannot dispute the fact that once wise men followed a star, now they follow the Son.

You cannot have an easily administered will when the language only whispers.

You cannot be acquitted from the person in the mirror.

You cannot have wisdom by never having doubt.

You cannot completely waste your day if you laugh a little.

You cannot own anything more valuable than knowledge.

You cannot fight a bear with a switch.

You cannot learn a better lesson from winning except to know you can.

You cannot have an hourglass figure unless you back away from the table.

You cannot stop talent from being a gift of passion and no one can stop it.

You cannot be rewarded at the bottom end of a golf club unless you do what you are supposed to do at the top end.

You cannot stop rumors from being faster communications than facts.

You cannot really grow up unless you learn how to act in public.

You cannot stretch loving arms any more than when they were on the cross.

You cannot babysit and clean a house at the same time.

You cannot give much better gifts than the ones you put in the offering plate.

You cannot stop optimists from looking for what is wrong and then figuring out a way to fix it.

You cannot easily break good habits.

You cannot eat like a hog and not become a butterball.

You cannot stop some people from loving you no matter how much you lie, deceive, and cheat.

You cannot prevent people from learning from others.

You cannot stop some people from having obedience when it doesn't seem to matter.

You cannot teach some people to say thank you.

You cannot have a good image unless you are unusual in some way.

You cannot drink a fifth on the fourth and expect to operate efficiently on the fifth.

You cannot have a more straight line to success than discipline.

You cannot catch nearly as many flies with vinegar as you can with honey.

You cannot prevent kind words from being short and sweet, but their echoes will last forever.

You cannot mistake knowledge for wisdom; one helps you make a living, the other helps you make a life.

You cannot be successful unless you take time to do so.

You cannot prevent losing your eyesight from being real bad, but losing your vision is worse.

You cannot have a second childhood if you never stopped acting like a child in the first one.

You cannot hold on to old grudges and not create more.

You cannot stop judges and jurors from giving unjustified awards and penalties.

You cannot have better security than God.

You cannot change things unless you change your attitude.

You cannot take too long to decide what you want to do with your life; if you do, you have already done it.

You cannot get the job done if you are too busy looking for ways to put it off.

You cannot set a good example with words alone; it takes action.

You cannot really know your brothers and sisters until you divide an estate with them.

You cannot become a hero unless someone else provides you the opportunity.

You cannot stop some parents from telling their children if they don't stop doing wrong that it will cloud up and rain all over them.

You cannot ever think that God sent a committee to save you; he sent his only Son.

You cannot prevent geniuses from knowing what they can or cannot do.

You cannot miss what you have never had.

You cannot stop the first half of your life from hearing your parents saying *"don't do that"* and the last half from telling your children to *"stop that."*

You cannot forget your enemies, but you can forgive them.

You cannot stop dentists from improving the *"sound bites"* of television reporters.

You cannot tell if a canary is a canary in a coal mine.

You cannot stop old men from having young girlfriends and wives, because women of their own age can see through them.

You cannot stop Pop from blowing a fuse when he gets the electric bill.

You cannot have a better wish than wishing for a new idea.

You cannot wind up where you want to be if you don't know where you want to go.

You cannot stop actions from reactions.

You cannot stop successful people from doing what unsuccessful people refuse to do.

You cannot stop some people from having an attention span any longer than that of a gnat.

You cannot become well informed unless you do diversified reading.

You cannot know when you might hit a good or bad golf shot.

You cannot get free admission to go to a better place than heaven.

You cannot get very far down the road on an ego trip.

You cannot have a need for an alarm clock when you have small children.

You cannot have inflation when your tire blows out.

You cannot have to eat your words if you hold your tongue.

You cannot lie in a beautiful apartment and overlook the rent.

You cannot get people to notice clean air until they don't have it.

You cannot stop some people from being real good at procrastination.

You cannot think you are being good to your children if you fail to give them discipline.

You cannot have a greater gift than the opportunity to go where you will live forever.

You cannot think you are being good to children if you fail to give them discipline.

You cannot stop some daycare centers from being better for children than their homes.

You cannot find people who dance on just one leg.

You cannot stop some parents from acting worse than their children.

You cannot stop things from being good or bad by comparison.

You cannot believe that you are the only person that suffers from loneliness.

You cannot let other people decide your priorities unless you decide to do so.

You cannot always pick your roommate; you may just have to take what is left.

You cannot tell when or where an itch will happen.

You cannot continue to walk if you don't walk.

You cannot juggle cotton balls in a windstorm.

You cannot stop a lot of boxers from losing their brain power.

You cannot be sure that the most you wish for will be the least you will get.

You cannot be two-faced and have both make an image in the mirror.

You cannot find many people who are willing to work hard enough to keep themselves educated.

You cannot continue to keep making the same mistakes and be considered smart.

You cannot burn your bridges unless you are a good swimmer.

You cannot win the respect of people if you lie to them.

You cannot trust a liar any more than you can a thief.

You cannot give up if you want to get up.

You cannot solve problems until you admit you have them.

You cannot find many teenagers who think their parents are right.

You cannot find a better friend than your dog.

You cannot plan the weather.

You cannot prevent bad things from happening to good people.

You cannot stop bees from stinging, even though they make good honey.

You cannot prevent later from being sooner than you think.

You cannot expedite your visit much faster than backing in the door.

You cannot appreciate another good day unless you try not having any.

You cannot convince an optimist that failure is an option.

You cannot spend yourself out of guilt.

You cannot be on the wrong road and the right road at the same time.

You cannot make a very big shadow when you have an hourglass figure.

You cannot have honesty with yourself unless you tell the truth to others.

You cannot stop status symbols from being poor excuses for real values.

You cannot get a real optimist to give up.

You cannot need much more exercise if you are pushing fifty.

You cannot make good decisions unless you have the proper knowledge.

You cannot prevent a small part of the body (the tongue) from getting you into big trouble.

You cannot stop people who laugh last from being slow thinkers.

You cannot be judged by your intentions, but you sure can by your actions.

You cannot stop half brothers and sisters from looking like whole people.

You cannot stop a lot of people from trying to blame their problems and mistakes on someone else; they just can't stand to blame the person they see in the mirror.

You cannot stop knowledge from being the results of hard work.

You cannot be sure that you will not find out that lettuce is fattening after all.

You cannot convince a motorcyclist that a *'lien holder'* is not a kickstand.

You cannot prevent some people from making things happen, while others just let things happen, and others wonder what happened.

You cannot use steps as a storage area and be safe from injury.

You cannot prevent some people's intelligence from being any deeper than floor wax.

You cannot be assured that brains and beauty come in the same package.

You cannot get a lot of young people to realize that they are making a mistake by not preparing for their retirement until they get old.

You cannot eat too many square meals and not get a round belly.

You cannot prevent some people from being so successful that they are lonely in a crowd.

You cannot stand up in a canoe and be safe unless you have on a life preserver.

You cannot prevent a bad attitude from being a serious disability.

You cannot get monkeys to turn loose of their limb until they know where the next limb is to cling to.

You cannot be the choice of thinking people and get a majority of the votes at the same time.

You cannot stop people from being victims of their own decisions.

You cannot find a more destructive weapon than the human tongue and brain.

You cannot get some people to answer your question without them asking you a question to answer your question.

You cannot get a lot of people to go by the whole truth; they go by half-truths and never take the time to search out the real truth.

You cannot direct the wind, but you can adjust your sails.

You cannot prevent doctors from having their mistakes buried.

You cannot find anything that will bind a family together better than love.

You cannot commit suicide and still not be considered a murderer.

You cannot tell what would have happened if you give up.

You cannot succeed unless you are unwilling to fail.

You cannot see the light unless you are willing to do what is right.

You cannot find a map that shows the state of shock.

You cannot find many people who are capable of total freedom.

You cannot stop some people from having a hopping good time at a party when they have a broken leg.

You cannot have a cap on your success unless you put it there.

You cannot always have enough knowledge to recognize your own ignorance.

You cannot make your measurements more accurate than your Ruler.

You cannot assume that violence will provide a satisfactory way to settle your differences with someone you disagree with.

You cannot fail to do your homework before you invest if you want to be a successful investor.

You cannot fake gravity.

You cannot get dogs to eat a certain brand of dog food just because it is highly advertised.

You cannot take the sting out of the bee just because it makes sweet-tasting honey.

You cannot stop golf from being a dumb game.

You cannot stop people from looking through their life filters and seeing only what they want to see.

You cannot be any more than what you know.

You cannot buy a good home; you have to make it.

You cannot prevent some people from causing pain to their brain if they sit down too hard.

You cannot waste anything any more valuable than a human mind.

You cannot risk more by not risking anything.

You cannot have integrity unless you tell yourself the truth.

You cannot win unless you believe you are worthy to win.

You cannot shoot the breeze even with a real gun.

You cannot stop other players from talking to your golf ball even if it has its hearing aid turned off.

You cannot find anything more uncommon than common sense.

You cannot keep your mind open unless you know when to keep your mouth shut.

You cannot see very well if you practice an eye for an eye.

You cannot un-ring a bell.

You cannot have a better surprise than when you surprise yourself.

You cannot lose your best friend if your best friend is your dog.

You cannot tell when to trust someone once you catch them lying.

You cannot be normal unless you are broke.

You cannot stop wills and trusts from causing family fights.

You cannot stop some people from being like fertilizer for doing what is wrong.

You cannot hide your lying eyes.

You cannot be sure there is always a Jack for every Jill.

You cannot prevent some forms of vision from improving with age.

You cannot find people that volunteer to fail.

You cannot do what is right as easy as you can what is easy.

You cannot find the middle of nowhere.

You cannot prevent sound from traveling real slow with teenagers; sometimes it takes 20 or 30 years for them to hear what their parents said to them.

You cannot stop courage from being the product of progress.

You cannot condemn the mirror for what it reflects.

You cannot find people who think skunks are welcome guests at lawn parties or picnics.

You cannot prevent flowers and plants from being silent while bringing good feelings.

You cannot prevent children from being like municipal bonds; they eventually mature.

You cannot explain to your wife on the way home why you thought all the women at the party thought you were handsome, sexy, and irresistible.

You cannot have a richer life than having the secret of how to have more beginnings than endings.

You cannot find anything that travels faster than light.

You cannot get your priorities (God, family and work) mixed up and come out ahead.

You cannot buy your way into the place you want to go when you die.

You cannot survive unless you maintain the three necessities of life ... *food, shelter, and clothing.* You almost need to add two more ... *utilities and transportation.*

You cannot prevent the past from being what really happened, but history is what someone wrote down.

You cannot say it is a mistake to have strong views, but to have nothing else is.

You cannot stop optimists from thinking we live in the best of all worlds, but pessimists fear it may be true.

You cannot have a better command of language than knowing when to keep your mouth shut.

You cannot always use gentle words to get your point across.

You cannot find anything that makes an itch feel as good as a scratch.

You cannot make progress to improve yourself unless you attempt to learn something new everyday.

You cannot stop life from having obstacle illusions.

You cannot use only ten percent of your brain unless you want to be average and ordinary.

You cannot prevent creative minds from surviving from bad training.

You cannot stop time from changing things.

You cannot stop books from sleeping under their covers or in their shelf.

You cannot discourage people who say there is a better way, let them find it.

You cannot stop change from changing.

You cannot take chances and win often unless you are smart.

You cannot get dead men or fools to change their minds.

You cannot marry your mistress and not create a vacancy in that position.

You cannot find limits on stupidity.

You cannot have plans that never change.

You cannot have a need for life insurance unless someone else is dependent on you for their livelihood.

You cannot convince some people from thinking their wants are necessities.

You cannot put your foot down if you do not have a leg to stand on.

You cannot prevent seven days without food from making one weak.

You cannot recover the fumble unless you are on the field.

You cannot learn very much from the second kick of a mule.

You cannot prevent playing golf from embarrassing you, humiliating you, and humbling your soul.

You cannot stop good pitching from stopping good hitting any more than you can stop good hitting from stopping good pitching.

You cannot get cards or dice to have memories.

You cannot be a Christian if you don't know what one is.

You cannot stop non-fools from benefiting and making money off of fools.

You cannot find a faster way to get more knowledge than to surround yourself with people who are smarter than you.

You cannot be rebellious and serve God.

You cannot stop average from being the best of the worst and the worst of the best.

You cannot stop the human brain from being the best and the greatest remote control in the world; just remember before any other remote control works, the brain had to do its work.

You cannot ignore the facts and get them to change.

You cannot get dizzy doing good turns.

You cannot find many people who want or need drill bits, but there are a lot of people who need holes.

You cannot find a more destructive force than the human mouth.

You cannot be the smartest person in the world and not believe in the Lord.

You cannot enjoy soaking unless you get in the water.

You cannot dishonor your mother and father and make your days be merry.

You cannot build good character by stealing, cheating and lying.

You cannot be very young when the candles on your birthday cake cost more than the cake.

You cannot stop age from creating wisdom.

You cannot stop getting to your wits end, but when you go, you will find that God lives there.

You cannot destroy your character by practicing integrity.

You cannot get lost in thought if you don't do any thinking.

You cannot buy lasting peace with the devil.

You cannot do wrong and not have to accept the consequences.

You cannot determine if any thing is equal, good or bad, except by comparison.

You cannot take your dirty laundry out of the hamper and make everyone happy.

You cannot prevent some people from graduating from obnoxious schools or universities.

You cannot put a value on our Savior or your own life.

You cannot find many people who are six feet above criticism.

You cannot stop some people from being kind, polite, and sweet-spirited until you try to sit in their pews.

You cannot stop children from needing more models than critics.

You cannot lose anything in life more valuable than to have people lose their trust in you.

You cannot prevent some people from performing acts that will damage their reputation for the rest of their lives that cannot be repaired.

You cannot set examples for young people by cheating, lying and stealing.

You cannot sell knowledge if you do not have it.

You cannot prevent education from showing that you are ignorant.

You cannot stop people who have the most birthdays from living the longest.

You cannot stop age from making wrinkles any more than you can stop it from creating wisdom.

You cannot prevent people from needing God to be their big eraser.

You cannot stop the phrase "and in conclusion" from waking up the audience.

You cannot do right by doing wrong.

You cannot live up to your principles nearly as easy as you can fight for them.

You cannot be sure that you have an education just because you have a diploma; there is a real difference.

You cannot stop goals from being dreams with deadlines.

You cannot always get opportunity to knock more than once, but temptation bangs on your front door constantly.

You cannot stop unity from having the same goals, but different opinions on how to obtain the same results.

You cannot stop people from wanting to serve God, but only as advisors.

You cannot say that the Lord did not have a purpose for creating every thing, but mosquitoes come very close.

You cannot find a better way to start peace than giving a smile.

You cannot stop some people's minds from being like concrete; thoroughly mixed up, but permanently set.

You cannot prevent knowledge from speaking, but wisdom listens.

You cannot fail to keep your heart and your head in the right direction if you never want to worry about your feet.

You cannot take your dirty laundry out of the hamper and make everyone happy.

You cannot stop a lot of people from preaching a lot of sermons, but many will not live by them.

You cannot stop some people from griping about their church, but if it had to be perfect, they could not belong.

You cannot find many people who are called to be pastors, lawyers or judges, but a lot of us are called to be witnesses.

You cannot stop rainy days from being fare weather for cab drivers.

You cannot stop divorce from making a lot of children very sad.

You cannot prevent a small rudder from turning a big ship.

You cannot find any race of people who have not at some time lived in slavery.

You cannot stop lazy people from getting their rest before they get tired.

You cannot stop greed and selfishness from causing wars.

You cannot have a better definition of insanity than thinking you can keep doing the same thing over and over and thinking you will come up with different results; the results will be the same.

You cannot find a right way to do something wrong.

You cannot stop life from being somewhat like a roll of toilet paper, the closer it gets to the end, the faster it goes.

You cannot make your words to tough and harsh for tomorrow you may have to eat them.

You cannot fail unless you go past the edge.

You cannot find a more destructive part of the human body than the mouth, except the human brain; it has the capacity for good or bad.

You cannot have a greater temptation of life than the lust of the body and mind.

You cannot have a greater choice in you life than the choice to accept Jesus Christ as your Savior.

You cannot triumph unless you put a little *'umph'* in it.

You cannot prevent some people from making success happen.

You cannot prevent great power from coming from forgiveness.

You cannot stop yourself from giving yourself experience.

You cannot prevent an investment in knowledge from paying the best interest and dividends.

You cannot stop people from going to heaven or hell, but you might be a contributing factor in the direction they take.

You cannot stop reactions from happening from actions.

You cannot be sure a divorce will make things better; it might make things worse.

You cannot find a better place to spend eternity than heaven and the admission is free.

You cannot fall in love with a leech unless you want to get stuck with having to accept the responsibilities of being stuck.

You cannot prevent experience from being the best way to remember.

You cannot be sure that your past days have been your best, since today is the best you will receive today.

You cannot expect to receive the reward unless you finish the race.

You cannot find buildings with more stories than libraries.

You cannot really be considered successful unless you leave this earth better than you found it.

You cannot prevent marriage from being an institution for people who want to be institutionalized.

You cannot hear light.

You cannot prevent moonshine from giving you blurred vision.

You cannot find people who can walk on water, but there are some who know where the rocks are.

You cannot get your prayers heard unless you know who you are talking to.

You cannot stop change from changing.

You cannot have a better reservation than when you make your right final destination.

You cannot see your Mama doing anything better than when she is teaching angels how to sleep.

You cannot replace wasted time.

You cannot have anything in your life that is not temporary, except God.

You cannot tap a new cab driver on his first day at work on his shoulder if he has been a hearse driver and not risk having a serious accident.

You cannot thank God for some things and God not know you are lying.

You cannot compare heart surgeons to motorcycle mechanics; if you think so, try to rebuild an engine while it is running.

You cannot stop some men from being like place mats; they only come to the table when food is available.

You cannot get conceit to make the one that has it sick.

You cannot stop friends from coming and going.

You cannot get many people to think faster than they talk.

You cannot prevent men from being born equal any more than you can keep them equal.

You cannot stop some people from doing a lot with a little.

You cannot see your friends in hell because it is dark.

You cannot stop losing ground if you are throwing mud at someone else.

You cannot stop God from being the good, bad and only weather maker.

You cannot prevent air or water from occurring naturally.

You cannot find a better way of learning than asking questions to people who are learned.

You cannot do a lot with what you don't have.

You cannot prevent the supreme gift of the artist from knowing when to stop.

You cannot prevent evil from winning if good men do nothing.

You cannot be good to your child by not giving them discipline and teaching them right from wrong.

You cannot prevent the pursuit of happiness from being a good life of work.

You cannot prevent reading, writing and arithmetic from being the basis from which all other education is arrived.

You cannot prevent prudent people from doing their job or project diligently.

You cannot find many people who will or can say to you, I will not lie to you, I will not steal from you, and I will do everything I say I will do and more.

You cannot stop some so-called intellectuals from using more words than necessary to explain what they do not know.

You cannot find many people that have tattoos who wish they didn't.

You cannot stop a lot of men from being like fine wine; it takes them too long to mature.

You cannot live a long life without reaching old age.

You cannot have a more inexpensive way of improving your looks than a smile.

You cannot mess with Mrs. Murphy unless you want to deal with Mr. Murphy's Law.

You cannot stop each day you live from making you one day closer to when you die.

You cannot get winners to want to change the rules; they just want to find a way to understand them better.

You cannot stop good decision makers from always being in demand.

You cannot change the results unless you are willing to change your behavior.

You cannot find anyone who can add more beauty to themselves for less money than wearing a smile.

You cannot prevent sarcasm from preventing you from making friends.

You cannot find a way to test your ethics any more than selling a used car.

You cannot prevent being in love from being a glorious two and a half minutes.

You cannot assume that couch potatoes eat a lot of potatoes.

You cannot sell ice to Eskimos.

You cannot prevent wisdom from being applied knowledge.

You cannot ask God to bless America unless America blesses God.

You cannot stop some golfers from throwing their clubs in the lake.

You cannot make things right if you do not know what is wrong.

You cannot stop handlebars from being very important to hold on to.

You cannot have a more valuable asset than time.

You cannot prevent some people from thinking wisdom teeth give them wisdom.

You cannot get hogs to smell like perfume.

You cannot stop a lot of men from having the same type of bellies as pots.

You cannot stop babies from needing a lot of changes.

You cannot stop a lot of collect phone calls from being made and recorded on Mother's day and Father's day.

You cannot prevent everything that happens on the golf course from making someone happy.

You cannot buy your way into heaven, but you can get in for free.

You cannot use up creativity; the more you try the more you create.

You cannot prevent reading from being the cause of achieving.

You cannot have an endless amount of time.

You cannot always spend your time wisely.

You cannot find anything more valuable than time.

You cannot find anything more worth fighting for than freedom.

You cannot stop food from tasting better when it is served with a smile.

You cannot get a better preacher unless you pray for the one you have.

You cannot stop the sins of fathers from visiting their children, but nowadays, the sins of our children are visited upon their fathers.

You cannot prevent education from being expensive until you get the bill for ignorance.

You cannot work hard and sit loose and not fall asleep.

You cannot stop education from being a good life-time investment.

You cannot see grass grow even if you watch it.

You cannot stop some people from griping when they know it will not do any good, or make things change or be better.

You cannot have patience unless you let your light shine after your fuse has blown.

You cannot be whole without a better half.

You cannot prevent the man upstairs from burning this place up; He just might move the sun 50,000 miles closer to earth.

You cannot generally find clean kitchens in restaurants that do not have clean restrooms.

You cannot recycle lost or wasted time.

You cannot stop golf shots from making some golfers sad and other golfers happy.

You cannot stop truth from standing by its self.

You cannot be happy even though you are the richest man in the cemetery.

You cannot have a greater truth than knowing you don't know.

You cannot stop friends from being interesting when they speak unless they keep talking about the same thing.

You cannot stop some people from having to go to the restroom when they see the waiter bringing the check.

You cannot stop some people from treating you in the same manner that you treat them.

You cannot have very good eyesight if you are constantly looking for trouble.

You cannot have a good day when your four year old tells you it is real hard to flush a grapefruit down the toilet.

You cannot have a good marriage by being obnoxious, insulting, and making smart remarks.

You cannot stop some people from attending school all of their lives on Sundays.

You cannot find marriages that neither husband nor wife has not done something wrong, so let the one that has not done something wrong speak first.

You cannot prevent divorces unless both sides are willing to give a little.

You cannot stop some people from going to domineering school and graduating with degrees.

You cannot stop men and women from getting divorces.

You cannot nurse a grudge and make it get better.

You cannot stop donuts from surrounding their holes.

You cannot get happy by leaving the nut you have by getting another nut that is worse.

You cannot find many words that have more meaning than self; look it up in the dictionary.

You cannot stay in your shell if your wife keeps egging you on.

You cannot leave a better legacy to the world than a well-educated family.

You cannot escape from a problem unless you get it solved.

You cannot stop people from burning daylight.

You cannot find but one Savior and He is ready to do His job at all times.

You cannot stop some people from telling the truth even if it hurts.

You cannot have enough time unless you are serving it.

You cannot prevent the lack of education from creating more poverty.

You cannot stop seven days without prayer from making one weak.

You cannot prevent the desire for freedom from being worth fighting wars to protect.

You cannot have a rainbow unless you have rain and sunshine.

You cannot make firewood from the tree of knowledge.

You cannot prevent God from being a great eraser.

You cannot win the rat race unless you want to be a rat.

You cannot stop some people from having no respect for telling the truth and how their lies adversely effect the people they lie to, but there is no way they can lie to the person they see in the mirror.

You cannot prevent the higher educated people from generally earning more income than the less educated.

You cannot have a more complete prayer than to thank the Lord for all of his blessings and to ask his forgiveness for all of your sins.

You cannot be very happy unless you make up your mind you will be.

You cannot have a good day when the weight of the candles causes your birthday cake to collapse.

You cannot discover new oceans if you spend all your time on sandy beaches or on the dock.

You cannot prevent the human brain from being the most powerful thing in the world and being able to do good for people; nor can you prevent it from being the most powerful thing in the world and able to do bad.

You cannot stop paying for not being educated.

You cannot stop hell from being created for those who do not accept Jesus Christ as their Savior.

You cannot prevent golf from being a game of controlled mistakes or mistake management.

You cannot prevent the road to success from having potholes that you must maneuver around.

You cannot prevent some people from not being good enough at math to count calories.

You cannot get your best friend to turn against you if your best friend is your dog.

You cannot stop some people from saying that senior adults are having senior moments when they forget something.

You cannot have a good day when you call suicide prevention and they put you on hold.

You cannot get dead fish to go up stream.

You cannot keep walking unless you keep walking.

You cannot take the blood pressure of a corpse.

You cannot prevent some people from having everything they want but not everything they need.

You cannot stop hate from doing more damage to the person it is stored in than the person it is poured on.

You cannot stop love from doing less good being stored than being poured.

You cannot prevent some people from having dirty hands even after they have been washed.

You cannot go wrong if you buy a good bed and good shoes because if you are not in one, you are in the other.

You cannot prevent shallow thinking men from depending on luck while deep thinkers design a plan and go by the plan.

You cannot have a wrong time to do the right thing.

You cannot prevent ignorance from always being busy.

You cannot stop the future from becoming obsolete.

You cannot take back the spoken word or the neglected opportunity.

You cannot prevent children from becoming adults as they realize they can be right but can also be wrong.

You cannot stop the blow of a whip from raising welts, but the blow of the tongue crushes bones.

You cannot amend or change the words that have already been spoken, so think before you speak.

You cannot live long enough to learn from all of your mistakes; you must also learn from the mistakes of others.

You cannot get your tongue tangled up with your eyetooth and see very good.

You cannot learn nearly as much when your mouth is open as you can when it is shut.

You cannot build up poor people by tearing down the rich.

You cannot stop people who have money from figuring out ways to get more.

You cannot stop the chief obstacle to the progress of the human race because it is the human race.

You cannot have to remember what you said if you tell the truth.

You cannot find anything that is opened more by mistake than the mouth.

You cannot stick your foot in your mouth if it is shut.

You cannot stop people from going to sleep watching on the future.

You cannot stop some parents from sub-contracting out their child raising duties.

You cannot learn anything you don't already know when you are talking.

You cannot stop some people from saving face by keeping their mouth shut.

You cannot seem to get the future to arrive on time.

You cannot be so important that the weather will not determine how many people will attend your funeral.

You cannot get experience until just after you need it.

You cannot stop mistakes from giving you knowledge to help prevent you from making future mistakes.

You cannot be doing your job as a parent if you fail to give your children discipline. (Discipline, not abuse)

You cannot stop some people from flattering themselves with their own eyes.

You cannot describe a hard drive in the 1900's the same way you do today.

You cannot make a long story short because when you say *"to make a long story short,"* it is already long.

You cannot stop efficiency from making life easier and less costly.

You cannot lay your keys down on tables and counters and not eventually lose them; keep them in your pocket or pocketbook when not in use.

You cannot stop computer hobbyists and golfers from being hackers.

You cannot stop farmers and sailors from making a living off the land.

You cannot stop some optimists from becoming rich by buying out pessimists.

You cannot be a real good mudslinger and stay out of the mud.

You cannot remain silent at some time and not be thought of as a fool, but if you open your mouth, you may prove you are.

You cannot always continue to be an heir.

You cannot be disappointed if you expect nothing and get it.

You cannot get the benefit of experience until you get old enough and get the opportunity to use it; or unless you can use the experience of someone else.

You cannot prevent some people from thinking they are thinking.

You cannot do people wrong if you live up to half of what masonry teaches.

You cannot cure crime at the electric chair, but you can at the high chair.

You cannot have a better golf handicap than honesty.

You cannot stop antiques from having modern prices.

You cannot spread dirt (gossip) without losing ground.

You cannot be a good bowler if you can't hear a pin drop.

You cannot always use someone else's brain, so why not try to educate yourself so you can use your own.

You cannot skate on thin ice and not get in hot water.

You cannot get by on good looks for much longer than 15 to 30 minutes; after that you better know something.

You cannot see eye to eye with your spouse if one of you is taller than the other.

You cannot get the dead to go to heaven first because the ones who are alive have a six-foot start.

You cannot lose something if you know where it is.

You cannot have liberty unless you are willing to give it to others.

You cannot prevent think tanks from being understaffed.

You cannot prevent a smile from being a curve that makes things straight.

You cannot tell some dogs to heel because they may bite you there.

You cannot have planned disobedience and not get in serious trouble.

You cannot be the first to face pain.

You cannot stop the Son from coming down.

You cannot find people who say I want to fail.

You cannot stop people from saying they have a pain in their back when it is just their kids aggravating them.

You cannot have an easy job doing the Lord's work in a city of pagans.

You cannot prevent life from taking the life out of you.

You cannot find many people living who have been buried alive.

You cannot be sent to prison for sing to loud in the church choir.

You cannot create more time.

You cannot do any better than your best.

You cannot stop time from flying when you throw a clock.

You cannot rest on the accomplishments of the past; the future is yet to come.

You cannot stumble if you are standing still.

You cannot do the impossible too quickly, but you can the difficult.

You cannot stop water from remembering where to run.

You cannot stop the have-nots from wanting to take away from the haves.

You cannot stop non-thinkers from getting a lot of help from thinkers.

You cannot stop some undertakers from being sorry when certain people die.

You cannot make mistakes nearly as fast as computers can.

You cannot get much done with people that say it cannot be done.

You cannot burn water.

You cannot expect anyone to believe in you until you first believe in yourself.

You cannot find things that are easy to do that are not also easy not to do.

You cannot distribute intelligence evenly.

You cannot make lasting changes with constant criticism.

You cannot criticize someone else for what you would do under the same circumstances.

You cannot get a good education watching a lot of the shows on television.

You cannot change your life unless you stop procrastinating and do something.

You cannot make fewer mistakes unless you get more experience.

You cannot prevent the mistakes you made yesterday, but you don't have to make the same mistakes today.

You cannot start over unless you want to.

You cannot call on the Man upstairs to help you if you don't know Him.

You cannot stop crime from growing by putting fertilizer on it in the form of leniency.

You cannot get your dreams to come true if you oversleep.

You cannot find many pearls unless you open a lot of shells.

You cannot stop interest from working day and night.

You cannot find food or service in fast food restaurants that are as good as their advertisements and commercials.

You cannot get some people to look up at any other time except when they are laying down.

You cannot expect things to change unless you are willing to change.

You cannot be sure you will live to obtain your life expectancy age as assumed in the latest mortality tables.

You cannot take a train off the track and expect it to go anywhere.

You cannot be free unless you discipline yourself.

You cannot go to the mountaintop unless you go through the valley first.

You cannot lend books and expect to get them back.

You cannot have what you want unless you help other people get what they want.

You cannot see a better way of showing your behavior than looking at yourself in the mirror.

You cannot turn on the electricity unless you throw the switch.

You cannot finish your education.

You cannot be overweight if you will just increase your height.

You cannot recognize the problem if you are the problem.

You cannot take step number two until you take step number one.

You cannot be too tough on yourself.

You cannot be successful unless you try.

You cannot succeed by just looking at what is right; you must look for what is wrong and correct it.

You cannot give up the best is yet to come.

You cannot have color unless you have light.

You cannot live longer than you will be dead.

You cannot have to get up if you stay up.

You cannot get pregnant by practicing abstinence.

You cannot get anything out of the pump unless you put something in the pump and prime it first.

You cannot ever be sure that success or failure is final.

You cannot generally go wrong if you follow the advice you give to others.

You cannot stop the wind from blowing harder at the top of the flagpole than at the bottom.

You cannot have enough learning unless you have a little education to mix with it.

You cannot get second thoughts to come first.

You cannot have what is right if all you are looking for is convenience.

You cannot have small pleasures unless you have big thoughts.

You cannot get things right unless you correct what is wrong.

You cannot have a vacant lot or vacant mind that does not collect rubbish.

You cannot lose if you serve well.

You cannot stop minority rule as long as you have newborns.

You cannot be a real man unless you keep your promises.

You cannot save a drowning man that is twenty feet away by throwing him a fifteen-foot rope.

You cannot know it all if you can't remember what you know.

You cannot say in person what you say behind people's backs; if you do, you may wind up with no one to talk to.

You cannot keep yourself from getting in a tight spot if your conduct is loose.

You cannot read and study too much if you want to be at the right place at the right time.

You cannot be real lucky unless you read, study, and practice a lot.

You cannot prevent good advice from falling on deaf ears.

You cannot have a 50 year old brain in a 20 year old body.

You cannot stop some people from being in bad company even if they are alone.

You cannot make truth out of date.

You cannot have as much conversation on what you know as you can on what you think.

You cannot have the best tomorrow unless you properly prepare today.

You cannot stop all uneducated people from using horse sense.

You cannot talk to the Man upstairs unless you know Him.

You cannot stop men from trying to rule other men.

You cannot stop men from being man's worst enemy.

You cannot hide ignorance; it has a way of exposing itself.

You cannot swallow your pride easily.

You cannot stop people from obligating themselves for entertainment that will make them retire in poverty.

You cannot be #1 if you are a follower; you have to be a leader.

You cannot stand for anything if you are always sitting on the fence.

You cannot prevent your mind from operating like a parachute as long as you let it be open.

You cannot get some people to believe a wet paint sign; they have to touch it.

You cannot promote prosperity by teaching children to waste.

You cannot pay for education but once, but you can continually pay for ignorance.

You cannot stop people from taking advantage of those who will let them.

You cannot stop paying for education if you don't have it, but you can pay for ignorance the rest of your life.

You cannot name any two books that come close to being as valuable as the Bible and the Dictionary; they are the most valuable books in the world.

You cannot stop some people from needing to be notched up a few notches to have as much sense as a fool.

You cannot find anything slicker than a snail.

You cannot find hogs that enjoy making you breakfast.

You cannot start to teach manners to children to early.

You cannot always perform and not error and be human, but to correct your error is divine.

You cannot prevent young people from having more questions than they have answers.

You cannot prevent old people from having more answers to questions than young people.

You cannot see grass when you are looking down in a casket, but you can see it when you are looking down.

You cannot teach golf balls anything; they are as dumb as a rock; they won't do what you tell them.

You cannot stop dogs from chasing cars and not being able to drive them if they catch them.

You cannot prevent the application of knowledge from creating power.

You cannot stop average from being the best of the worst and the worst of the best.

You cannot bite the hand that feeds you unless you want to feel the pain that bites you back forever.

You cannot create fresh insults and not create bigger enemies.

You cannot promote inefficiency at your work and advance yourself or your employer.

You cannot get turtles to make progress unless they stick out their necks.

You cannot have anything any more welcome than a rain shower in the desert.

You cannot make yourself more effective except through talking, doing, other people, and writing.

You cannot lead people in silent prayer if people don't know how to pray.

You cannot stop people from stealing and giving.

You cannot read the newspaper without glasses when you get old because your arms do not grow long enough.

You cannot make your dreams come true unless you wake up.

You cannot stop learning from hard knocks, but books help.

You cannot play good golf with slick grips.

You cannot prevent failure if you fail to communicate.

You cannot get most people to listen; that is why history always repeats itself.

You cannot help your children any more than not being dependent on them when you get old.

You cannot be good to a child unless you give the child discipline.

You cannot find people who have no character flaws; some are just much more severe than others.

You cannot just be a talker to get anything done; you have got to be a doer.

You cannot finish first if you are timid, stand-offish and non-assertive; you must charge.

You cannot stop life from happening.

You cannot be *'a part'* if you are apart.

You cannot find anyone who has died as our substitute except for Jesus Christ.

You cannot find a game that will embarrass you, humiliate you, or humble your soul any more than golf.

You cannot get deep impressions from shallow speakers.

You cannot outlive all your friends if you have enough of them.

You cannot see to far down the road because the world is round.

You cannot learn enough from books; it takes years too.

You cannot stop time from slipping away.

You cannot stop men from having more expensive play toys than women.

You cannot stop women from living longer than men until men learn how to take care of themselves better.

You cannot be ashamed to ask unless you are afraid to learn from others.

You cannot get a person's real opinion of you unless you make them mad.

You cannot always give believable excuses; after a while, they are just excuses.

You cannot go to hell for telling the truth, but you can for lying.

You cannot ever expect people to trust you if they catch you lying.

You cannot have true love unless you give true love.

You cannot have wisdom unless you have had inexperience.

You cannot think of adults as anything except obsolete children.

You cannot pay too much to be educated, but you can to be amused.

You cannot notice men taking care of nature more than when you see them standing close to a tree.

You cannot have everything right until you take away everything that is wrong.

You cannot be any more committed than the hog was when he made the bacon.

You cannot find a golfer who does not think golf balls have ears.

You cannot find new oceans unless you are willing to lose sight of land.

You cannot stop dogs from hiking a hind leg when they come to a fire hydrant.

You cannot have greatness without some simplicity.

You cannot have a real wide conversation by saying what you know, but you can if you say what you think.

You cannot be afraid to ask questions if you want to learn.

You cannot say what you ought to say and keep your friends at the same time.

You cannot avoid an apology if you have done wrong and you want to keep your friends.

You cannot have all sunshine and not have a desert.

You cannot have tenure and come up with the most new ideas at the same time.

You cannot stop counting down from being a good way to stop blasting off.

You cannot keep lying unless you want your nose to get longer.

81

You cannot compromise if you want the top of the line.

You cannot get a good drink of water unless you go to the head of the stream.

You cannot avoid or ignore things and expect them to just go away.

You cannot see failure as failure; it is just a new learning experience.

You cannot have a better marriage unless you try.

You cannot listen very well when you are talking.

You cannot find the road to easy street unless you go through the sewer first.

You cannot choose your parents; in fact, you may not even know who they are.

You cannot have to remember what you said if you tell the truth.

You cannot own anything more expensive than ignorance.

You cannot find anyone who knows less than the person who knows everything.

You cannot loan out your books and expect to get them all back.

You cannot cheat the school if you don't get all the education they offer to let you have.

You cannot cheat the school if you don't get all of the education that you or your parents pay for.

You cannot cheat the school if you leave any of the education there instead of taking it with you.

You cannot swallow a frog if you look at it too long.

You cannot be overweight unless you decide to.

You cannot pay too much for education, but you can for being dumb.

You cannot need more than just the right amount of anything.

You cannot find golfers who do not talk to themselves.

You cannot go on a much better diet than using just one Chinese chopstick.

You cannot get ahead if you are just trying to stay even.

You cannot lie to an employer and act like an employee.

You cannot have a zero golf handicap and run a full time business to.

You cannot play good golf unless you play with old balls.

You cannot succeed if you do not try.

You cannot get fruit to fall very far from the tree.

You cannot stop your fingers from making points.

You cannot play good golf with slick grips.

You cannot tell when you will be punished for a good deed.

You cannot trust a liar any more than you can a thief.

You cannot enjoy change any more than a wet baby.

You cannot get ahead unless you take some chances.

You cannot magnify your own weaknesses as easily as you can someone else's.

You cannot live longer just because you have a nagging spouse; it just seems that way.

You cannot set a good example for your kids to live by unless you live the way you would have them to live.

You cannot have better birth control than abstinence.

You cannot wait to teach a child right from wrong if you want them to know.

You cannot stop dieters from being thick and tired of it.

You cannot be a fair judge unless you have heard both sides.

You cannot see the scenery change if you are not the lead dog.

You cannot be denied success if you are a go-getter.

You cannot find any better fat than the fat that makes up part of your own body.

You cannot regain the time you wasted.

You cannot prevent knowledge from being the frontier of tomorrow.

You cannot invent more time.

You cannot prevent knowing the truth about yourself.

You cannot prevent today's vision from being tomorrow's future.

You cannot overcome fear without knowledge.

You cannot have better antiques than old friends.

You cannot wait until you get thirsty to dig your well.

You cannot stop paying for education if you are uneducated.

You cannot put the fox in the hen house and also get eggs.

You cannot prevent your funeral from shrinking if it rains.

You cannot create success and be a reasonable person.

You cannot eat your cake and have it, too.

You cannot get very good experience doing nothing.

You cannot start too late to be what you should have been.

You cannot shut the door to new ideas if you don't want them to fly out the window.

You cannot have much experience when you are young, but it is a good time to get started.

You cannot worry about what people think about you because they really don't care about you.

You cannot stop paying for ignorance.

You cannot prevent the worst ink from being better than the best memory.

You cannot benefit from your knowledge unless you apply it.

You cannot stop time from flying.

You cannot heal a broken heart with anything but love and time.

You cannot know when a good deed will be punished.

You cannot find harder work than thinking; that is why so many people don't do it.

You cannot prevent your children from marrying weird people.

You cannot be sure that a man is a man or a woman is a woman.

You cannot stop little black books from getting you in trouble.

You cannot miss your mind if you lose it.

You cannot think nearly as well with your mouth open as you can with it shut.

You cannot stop asking questions if you want to continue to learn.

You cannot stop pessimist from looking for a casket when they smell flowers.

You cannot have a higher virtue than telling the truth.

You cannot stop the orchestra leader from turning his back to the crowd.

You cannot stop the future from coming soon enough.

You cannot stop some people's minds from growing even though their body stops.

You cannot prevent some people from telling the truth and doing what's right.

You cannot find old gun fighters.

You cannot prevent you children from doing nothing to help take care of you in your old age.

You cannot catch any fish if you are too busy cutting bait.

You cannot get mud on your hands when you are reaching for the stars.

You cannot blow your stack with polluting the air.

You cannot find a book to read that is more fun than the book you are reading.

You cannot find a better discovery than the one Columbus discovered.

You cannot help others if you are only surviving yourself.

You cannot x-ray some people between the ears and see anything.

You cannot have a better idea on lawyers than Shakespeare had.

You cannot be dead between the ears and accomplish much.

You cannot be wrong and be all alone.

You cannot settle for less than you deserve if you want to get what you deserve.

You cannot stop the people you love from putting you down the most.

You cannot stretch your mind and expect it to go back to its original dimension.

You cannot distort the facts unless you know what they are.

You cannot keep you life shining like a beacon if you don't keep your light on.

You cannot prevent some people from needing to read the book *Winning Friends and Influencing People*.

You cannot get rid of a fat brain by exercising it.

You cannot look at the green grass nearly as long as you can the brown roots.

You cannot help others if you are only surviving yourself.

You cannot find anything any more unique than a snowflake.

You cannot make good soup out of roses even if they do smell good.

You cannot build your character by failing and quitting the first time, but you can if you try four or five times.

You cannot change children unless you change the children's parents first.

You cannot train a dog or a child without consistency.

You cannot stop pessimists from saying *"I told you so"* when things don't go right.

You cannot find a better book for you to read than the Bible.

You cannot always hit perfection because it is a moving target.

You cannot prevent some women from getting black belts in shopping.

You cannot prevent knowledge and action from creating success.

You cannot prevent successful multilevel marketing from being based on the failure of a lot of people.

You cannot practice wrong and get perfect.

You cannot be required to look amazing to do amazing things.

You cannot prevent some birds from flying sideways.

You cannot prevent arguments from having three sides; your side, my side, and the right side.

You cannot have a solution that comes from an excuse.

You cannot get educated too soon to enjoy the fruits of life.

You cannot prevent experience from being the best way to eliminate mistakes.

You cannot be somebody unless you are more specific of who you want to be.

You cannot solve problems with hot heads and cold hearts.

You cannot stop practicing unless you want to get beat.

You cannot stop wise men from learning from fools.

You cannot always be sure which bridge to burn or which bridge to cross.

You cannot prevent people you supervise from calling you Boss, but if you don't treat them right, they spell Boss backwards.

You cannot stop luck from changing.

You cannot find a better architect than the Great Architect of the Universe.

You cannot prevent dumb people from being dependent on people who are not dumb.

You cannot find any race of people who have a monopoly on being good or bad.

You cannot stop anything from being more productive than the human mind.

You cannot predict the future unless you create it.

You cannot lose anything by discarding your faults.

You cannot stop good and bad from rubbing off.

You cannot stop wickedness from being weakness.

You cannot have tattoos removed for the low price you had them put on.

You cannot stop Murphy's Law from working, '*What can go wrong will,*' but you can have a contingency plan in place when it does.

You cannot keep doing the same things over and over and expecting different results; that is insanity.

You cannot prevent learning from being a life-long process.

You cannot break the law when stealing a base while playing baseball.

You cannot have freedom without responsibilities.

You cannot be delayed by a traffic jam on the road to heaven.

You cannot stop alcohol from causing lots of pain, suffering, fun, and fellowship.

You cannot prevent today's children from being tomorrow's voters and leaders.

You cannot prevent the pen from being mightier than the tongue or sword.

You cannot stop some people from playing too much football without a helmet.

You cannot stop the mind from obtaining more knowledge than you use.

You cannot improve on perfection.

You cannot prevent the room for improvement from being the biggest room in the house.

You cannot get anyone to give you good character; you have to learn it a little bit at a time.

You cannot find many people who cannot scream loud enough to hurt your ears.

You cannot stop running out of time.

You cannot prevent it from being nice to be important, but it is more important to be nice.

You cannot fail until you give up.

You cannot prevent forbidden fruit from getting a lot of people into a bad jam.

You cannot stop frogs from eating the bugs that bug them.

You cannot necessarily think when the going gets easy that you may be going downhill.

You cannot get good exercise by jumping to bad conclusions.

You cannot prevent failure if you have no persistence.

You cannot always be at the right place at the right time.

You cannot be at the right place at the right time too often.

You cannot please everybody doing the right thing.

You cannot have a happy marriage by having yours and mine; it must be ours.

You cannot have a smooth ride unless you have a round wheel.

You cannot make two parallel lines meet.

You cannot give up just because the going gets tough.

You cannot do it better unless you find a better way.

You cannot create class hatred without being hated.

You cannot under educate and improve the standard of living.

You cannot get ahead walking around in chains.

You cannot have a rainbow without a little rain.

You cannot lie about how low your golf handicap is and not shoot above your handicap.

You cannot stop making friends before you need them if you want to have any when you do.

You cannot finish unless you have the courage to start.

You cannot find near as many faults looking through a telescope as you can looking in a mirror.

You cannot prevent short words from being easily spoken.

You cannot prevent kind words from having good echoes.

You cannot prevent people from doing what's right; they do not live forever.

You cannot find others who can change your life; they can only give you the information for you to change your life.

You cannot get many people to do the unpleasant things long enough to be able to receive the pleasant things.

You cannot stretch the truth unless you are ready to receive the snapback.

You cannot have a bigger change in your life than walking down the aisle.

You cannot have a more happy labor than the one you have for a wanted child.

You cannot prevent people who sling mud from eventually losing ground.

You cannot stop opportunity from knocking, but you have to open the door.

You cannot have a better gift than learning, but it is not complete unless you pass it on.

You cannot prevent valuable knowledge from being stored in minds and books.

You cannot be exposed any more than being a worm on the ground in the middle of a flock of birds on the ground.

You cannot get some preachers to realize that their sermons are like biscuits; they need more shortening.

You cannot build character with sports, but sports will reveal your character.

You cannot become famous for what you say until you become famous for what you have done.

You cannot be a real bad magician if you can pull love out of your own hat.

You cannot think clearly with clinched fists.

You cannot be tactful if you are to busy belittling.

You cannot have a rainbow unless you have a little rain.

You cannot hear people thinking.

You cannot stop achievements from raising one's level of expectation.

You cannot stop being slobbered on when you get in the doghouse.

You cannot stop silence from sending a loud message.

You cannot have all your distractions in front of you when you are driving a school bus.

You cannot stop shaking your leg unless you want to let someone pull it.

You cannot stop incompetence from causing problems.

You cannot prevent your mistakes from being worthwhile if you learn from them.

You cannot stop scam artist from using suckers as canvas.

You cannot stop wild birds from working; they have to eat.

You cannot win a race that you do not enter.

You cannot find many people who can handle total freedom.

You cannot know if you don't know.

You cannot stay in good shape unless you get some kind of exercise.

You cannot go very far wrong doing what is right.

You cannot blame the beer, liquor, and winemakers for your alcohol addiction.

You cannot spoil a good walk by playing a little golf on the way.

You cannot stop maturity from being a high price to pay for growing up.

You cannot stop people from substituting opinions for facts.

You cannot stop consequences from being the results of your decisions.

You cannot need more time to tell what you know than what you think.

You cannot shrink your mind if you have stretched it with new ideas.

You cannot stop controlling your life and almost everything that happens in it.

You cannot find many people who know the difference between wants and needs.

You cannot get anywhere if you don't stick your neck out; that is how turtles find out where they are.

You cannot get time back that you wasted; so spend it wisely.

You cannot find failures that plan to fail; they just failed to plan.

You cannot unbreak an egg.

You cannot find many people who will say, *"I will take care of it."*

You cannot stop incompetent people from making trouble for both themselves and others.

You cannot find many men that eat and then run.

You cannot put toothpaste back in the tube.

You cannot depend on a rabbit's foot to bring you good luck; think about what happened to the rabbit.

You cannot find an oversupply of moral courage.

You cannot stop good acts from building friends any more than you can stop one bad act from losing them.

You cannot make a bigger mistake than doing nothing.

You cannot stop ideas from being worthless unless you put them into action.

You cannot get ahead unless you do more than the minimum.

You cannot stop good habits from being addictive any more than you can bad ones.

You cannot be charged with plagiarism if you steal from a lot of writers, but you can if you steal from just one.

You cannot prevent education from surviving; it has eternal life.

You cannot realize the pleasure of real pain until you have a baby.

You cannot let your children know how you learned about the things you tell them not to do.

You cannot have a good idea unless you put it to work.

You cannot get the dead to hear the compliment you failed to make when they were alive.

You cannot find a better time to start to be successful than now.

You cannot learn as much talking as you can by listening; that is the reason the Lord gave you two ears and only one mouth.

You cannot stop goals from being more productive than dreams.

You cannot dress like a turkey if you want to impress people that you are an eagle.

You cannot expect teachers to teach kids when all they have time to do is try to have discipline and order.

You cannot teach your children how to get along without you until they need you.

You cannot stop success from making your ego grow.

You cannot stop knowledge from increasing.

You cannot kill time; it has eternal life.

You cannot follow the teachings of the prince of darkness and learn how to treat people the way they should be treated.

You cannot make any more air.

You cannot play good golf without some good luck.

You cannot be afraid to ask if you want to learn.

You cannot smoke a real long time if you smoke.

You cannot be committing a sin when you are cheating the devil.

You cannot make any more water.

You cannot prevent our conduct from being the results of our character.

You cannot make many mistakes if you measure ten times and cut once.

You cannot make any more sunlight.

You cannot find anything that gets more attention than good and bad.

You cannot stop kudzu from multiplying overnight.

You cannot find the answers to your problem in the bottom of a beer can or whiskey bottle.

You cannot have better troubles than little ones.

You cannot make any more moonlight.

You cannot go forward backing up.

You cannot increase your ability for success unless you increase your vocabulary.

You cannot stop time from being slippery.

You cannot have a good tomorrow unless you prepare for it today.

You cannot have too many birthdays if you live long enough.

You cannot tell a smart aleck very much.

You cannot be unwise from sometimes unlearning some of the things you have learned.

You cannot have any better planning than Noah had.

You cannot say *"Lord have mercy"* and it do any good unless you know who you are talking to.

You cannot save everything in your two-car garage and have room for two cars.

You cannot stay out of hell if you are mean to old people and babies.

You cannot have any better love than true love.

You cannot make a putt if you leave it short.

You cannot prevent children from learning evil if they watch enough television.

You cannot say television has not been one of the greatest inventions known to mankind, but by the same token, you cannot say it has not been one of the worst.

You cannot expect children to learn right from wrong without help from their parents.

You cannot expect children to respect right from wrong when their parents have no respect for what is right or wrong.

You cannot get out of a hole if you keep digging the hole deeper.

You cannot stay educated if you stop educating yourself when you get out of school.

You cannot have near as good of an opinion as you can if you have had actual experience.

You cannot be sure a good deed will not go unnoticed.

You cannot teach kids bad habits if you keep them chasing a ball.

You cannot stop changing your mind if you have one.

You cannot depreciate knowledge; it appreciates with age.

You cannot have secrets and keep a diary, too.

You cannot expect your children to help you; they are too busy figuring out ways for you to help them.

You cannot take advantage of people and not eventually get caught.

You cannot stop winners from being prepared to win.

You cannot be insulting, obnoxious or sarcastic and have many friends; you might try reading the book, *How to Win Friends and Influence People*.

You cannot win with negatives; it creates losers.

You cannot prevent maturity from being a high price for growing up.

You cannot get hot flashes if you are a man.

You cannot have more fun than loving what you do.

You cannot prevent mistakes from giving you self-education.

You cannot get your good intentions to be helpful unless you put them into effect.

You cannot stop the wise from doing in the beginning what fools do in the end.

You cannot stop people from sounding convincing when they are telling the truth.

You cannot prevent misers from making great ancestors.

You cannot find people who mind criticism as long as it is not about them.

You cannot get some of your friends to take or go by your advice even when it is right.

You cannot graduate from Sunday school.

You cannot stop some people from claiming their pew even after they are dead and gone.

You cannot stop character from being what you are when no one else is looking.

You cannot stop some people from being like rose stems; if you fool with them, you will get stuck.

You cannot stop men from looking at women with short skirts and low cut tops.

You cannot prevent some people from already knowing a lot of these *You Cannots*, but this book will serve as a good reminder.

You cannot prevent the difference between good and great from being a little bit extra.

You cannot destroy true love.

You cannot build good character when you lie, cheat and steal.

You cannot stop hate with more hate.

You cannot stop some people from thinking winning is everything even if it is done unfairly and unethically, even though others think it should be done fairly and ethically?

You cannot prevent some people from becoming as unequal as they want to be.

You cannot find the time you lost.

You cannot hit a home run unless you get past third base.

You cannot get the fat lady to sing unless she has something to sing about.

You cannot have a multiple choice on which of the Ten Commandments you should obey.

You cannot get indigestion from swallowing your pride.

You cannot change your life unless you are willing to change.

You cannot show insanity any better than to keep on doing the same thing over and over and expecting different results.

You cannot use people and throw them away like paper cups and not eventually get used and thrown away like a paper cup.

You cannot realize how much education is worth unless you have it.

You cannot squeeze the handle on a coffee pot and get more coffee.

You cannot keep snow from getting bigger by rolling it.

You cannot present a good sermon unless you set a good example.

You cannot stop some men from being like a hammer; not much change in the last two thousand years, but handy to have around.

You cannot stop the best things in life from being free. Such as, but not limited to, air, daylight, dark, rain, warm weather, cold weather, snow, blue skies, and sunshine.

You cannot get much done if you work like a dog.

You cannot explain well enough to keep people from saying, "what if".

You cannot stop men and women from being like subways; they use the same old pickup lines.

You cannot stop a lot of people from being like an hourglass; over time their weight shifts to the bottom.

You cannot stop those who refuse to learn from history from being condemned when it repeats itself.

You cannot stop Ziploc bags from holding a lot of things, but you can see right through them.

You cannot stop men from being like unpolished shoes with their tongues hanging out.

You cannot stop lazy men from being like hot air balloons; you have to light a fire under them to get them started.

You cannot stop some people from saying you have already told that story twice today.

You cannot dig yourself out of your grave if you are buried face down.

You cannot stop some people from having dirty hands even after they have been washed.

You cannot mix high speed and wet roads and not create danger.

You cannot prevent yourself from being smarter than some others, but you need to continue to be so by not telling them.

You cannot handle temptation without help.

You cannot do anything without the help from someone.

You cannot fail to get an appointment with God; he always has an opening.

You cannot prevent some people from needing brain food.

You cannot stop some people from griping and complaining about doing something they intend to do.

You cannot take a greater gamble than not accepting the Lord as your Savior.

You cannot get mosquitoes to know where to start when they are in a nudist colony.

You cannot enjoy the cider as much unless you peel the apples.

You cannot always be sure the person behind the steering wheel is driving the car; they may be sitting in the passenger seat or the back seat.

You cannot always bury your sorrows; they have a way of coming back.

You cannot be happy with what you get for nothing.

You cannot take more out of this world than you brought into it.

You cannot determine the time between life and death.

You cannot continue to ignore road warning signs and not maybe end up where you don't want to be.

You cannot ignore road warning signs in the Bible and have an everlasting life.

You cannot get people to say that some things aggravate the dark out of them.

You cannot need to do anything in life except what is right.

You cannot always sit under the trees you plant.

You cannot stop a good scare from being better than good advice.

You cannot get trouble that you invite to reject your invitation.

You cannot get evil words that are swallowed and not said to give you a stomachache.

You cannot prevent God from allowing U-turns.

You cannot stop people from saying that some things aggravate the daylights out of them.

You cannot prevent people from having the right to be wrong.

You cannot stop life from giving you the test before you have had time to study the lesson.

You cannot prevent good fruit from growing toward the end of the limb.

You cannot hit rock bottom and not be on solid ground.

You cannot stop receiving joy when you give more than you receive.

You cannot stop some people from trying to ride a dead horse.

You cannot stop a lot of these *You Cannots* from being just good common horse sense.

You cannot stop golf grips from collecting oil from your hands and causing them to get slick, but you can get a Matlock Golf Grip Washer that will make them feel new, clean and tacky.

You cannot stop some people from being obnoxious and sarcastic; it just comes naturally and they see nothing wrong.

You cannot stop a lot of people from saying I can't, but you will find some that say I can and I will find a way; these are the people who make progress.

You cannot find many other family members who will approve of grandmothers showing favoritism to her favorite grandchildren.

You cannot prevent getting a hot foot if you walk on hot coals.

You cannot stop people who hang around with losers from not becoming losers.

You cannot prevent birds of a feather from flocking together.

You cannot stop dentists from having filling stations.

You cannot stop some people from being dog tired at the end of the day because they have growled all day long.

You cannot prevent people who are over the hill from picking up speed.

You cannot stop bees from flying even though aerodynamics laws say they can't.

You cannot stop love and hate from being four letter words.

You cannot get men to very easily admit to bad judgment near as much as bad memory.

You cannot get the job done of quitting smoking if there are ifs, ands, and butts.

You cannot stop people from going on see-food diets; they see food and eat it.

You cannot prevent the legs on three legged stools from having equal responsibility.

You cannot stop luck from changing.

You cannot do very much, but we can.

You cannot find anyone in the position to look down on everyone except God.

You cannot have or maintain freedom for free; it has a price.

You cannot get character to be a gift; it has to be earned a little at the time.

You cannot get much luck without a lot of preparation.

You cannot stop some people from thinking they are in love when they think a pimple is a dimple.

You cannot stop friends from being like houseplants; they require a lot of care.

You cannot stop a lot of people from having two choices for dinner; '*take it*' or '*leave it*'.

You cannot know the true character of a person unless you share an inheritance with that person.

You cannot guard you soul unless you tame your tongue.

You cannot have self-esteem unless you are tough.

You cannot know what a fool you are until you hear yourself being imitated by one.

You cannot sleep in a bed better than your own.

You cannot stop wise boys and girls from making moms and dads feel proud.

You cannot have anything better to happen to you than getting old; and you cannot stop it from being in the middle of life.

You cannot stop a lot of people from getting too much elbow exercise.

You cannot get a closed mouth to get a foot stuck in it.

You cannot have a better blessing than to have parents that just teach you to just do what is right.

You cannot prevent some kids from being spoiled, even though they do not smell bad.

You cannot prevent some people from accepting an eye for an eye.

You cannot tell where wind comes from.

You cannot stop food that melts in your mouth from turning solid on your waistline.

You cannot stop the sun from rising in the east and setting in the west.

You cannot find anyone that has made a light that gives off more light than the moon.

You cannot stop people from going to hell or heaven.

You cannot be expected to do anything except to do what is right.

You cannot hide light.

You cannot get time to stay still.

You cannot stop some people from being kinder when they find fault with others.

You cannot stop knowledge from creating power.

You cannot stop some people from thinking the best thing they can hope for is disappointment.

You cannot find a better world heater than the sun.

You cannot stop the author, Roy Matlock, Sr., from writing some of his *You Cannots* more than once; it just makes them sink-in.

You cannot stop Murphy's Law; what can go wrong will at some time.

You cannot stop water from saving your life or taking your life away.

You cannot keep a secret if you tell anyone.

You cannot build old friendships overnight.

You cannot stop sporting events from having most of the coaches in the stands.

You cannot stop some people from having to eat their own words.

You cannot stop light from being faster than sound.

You cannot stop small seeds from growing big plants.

You cannot have anything better to happen to you than getting old.

You cannot stop some people from being in pretty good shape for the shape they are in.

You cannot stop revenge from being a poor way to show your character.

You cannot stop some people from doing what other people think is impossible.

You cannot stop the sun and moon from shining.

You cannot stop people from backsliding.

You cannot stop education from being a ladder to gather fruit from trees.

You cannot tease your hair unless you want it to look irritated.

You cannot freeze the wages of sin.

You cannot stop people from getting wise too late and old too soon.

You cannot make any more water.

You cannot take on more calories than when you have to eat your own words.

You cannot stop learning when you finish school, because that is just the beginning.

You cannot teach your children all they need to know unless you teach them how to get along without *us*.

You cannot prevent your sheep from being on the lam if you are a shepherd and can't find them.

You cannot live very well from the fortune you get from fortune cookies.

You cannot stop golf from being played between the ears.

You cannot stop people from saying who shot John even if John has never been shot.

You cannot stop things that are worth doing from not being done.

You cannot make any new old friends.

You cannot hang on to a basketball rim without being suspended.

You cannot find a better designer than God

You cannot find the four corners of a round world.

You cannot see the forest because the trees get in the way.

You cannot control the uncontrollable.

You cannot give your tired legs a better rest than kneeling.

You cannot stop outward signs from showing inward change.

You cannot fail to read good books and be any better off than the person that cannot read.

You cannot have better security than eternal security.

You cannot control or prevent hurricanes or other storms.

You cannot easily explain colors to a blind person.

You cannot stop smoking from being a grave issue.

111

You cannot stop committees from saving minutes and wasting hours.

You cannot stop '*control*' from being very powerful.

You cannot be wrong if you stay silent at the right time.

You cannot find the ladder for success if you are waiting for the elevator.

You cannot stop schools from making people think.

You cannot stop optimist from taking advantage of deals that pessimist turn down.

You cannot stop the tongue from being small and weak, but having enough power to change the world.

You cannot stop a lot of overweight people from getting too much elbow exercise.

You cannot stop people's bodies from showing that they are getting too much or just the right amount of elbow exercise.

You cannot stop greed and selfishness from causing a lot of fights and wards.

You cannot stop education from making you what you are.

You cannot find shade trees along the side of the road to success.

You cannot find many men who have worn out a necktie.

You cannot stop geniuses from skipping generations.

You cannot stop what you know from being valuable if what you know is the right thing to do.

You cannot overlook your mistakes if you do not want to repeat them.

You cannot prevent the author, Roy L. Matlock, Sr., from having a loss of memory and writing the same *You Cannots* more than one time. He is just trying to make you enjoy them more.

You cannot stop a happy marriage if you keep your mouth shut and your checkbook open.

You cannot stop desire from being the starting point for success.

You cannot think you can if you think you can't.

You cannot steal someone's thunder they never had.

You cannot stop some people from being so bad that even Satan does not want them.

You cannot fail to respect yourself if you want to get respect from others.

You cannot tell the difference between broad daylight and other daylight.

You cannot tell the difference between a country mile and any other mile.

You cannot have winners without losers.

You cannot realize how many faults you have until you get married.

You cannot carry a heavier load on your shoulder than a chip.

You cannot get people that can or can't swim to walk on water.

You cannot find people that build icebergs.

You cannot stop silent and listen from being spelled with the same letters.

You cannot find people who are full of bologna.

You cannot stop people from becoming learned or unlearned.

You cannot stop people from digging their own graves with forks and knives.

You cannot stop children from getting smarter as their parents get older.

You cannot find anything more dangerous than ignorance.

You cannot find anything more educationally important than adding, subtracting, multiplying and dividing.

You cannot build a reputation near as fast as you can destroy it.

You cannot stop people from saying their heart just stood still, but they better hope it doesn't.

You cannot know too much to make a wise decision.

You cannot walk on water just because you ride a wave.

You cannot have as much fun in the daytime as you can at night.

You cannot make a mistake if you never try anything new.

You cannot get some people to drink from the fountain of knowledge; they just gargle.

You cannot stop some people's success from going to their mouth instead of their head.

You cannot stop doctors from having patients.

You cannot stop people who have part of their colon removed from having a semicolon.

You cannot grow food on the mountain top, but you can in the valley.

You cannot sit on a two-legged stool and be very comfortable.

You cannot stop pessimistic people from having B-negative blood types.

You cannot meet a winner that was not at some time a beginner.

You cannot find people who look up that are depressed.

You cannot stop words from changing your behavior.

You cannot say that you do not believe in gravity unless you are willing to jump off of a ten-story building with no parachute or net.

You cannot stop sick people or ships from going to the dock.

You cannot have an opportunity to do more than when you are doing nothing.

You cannot speak in anger and not give a speech you will not want to remember.

You cannot sneeze with your eyes open.

You cannot stop wolves and sheep from wanting different diets.

You cannot stop children from having a dog that can jump higher than a horse.

You cannot tell the strength of a man or woman until they get in hot water.

You cannot rearrange your prejudice unless you do some thinking.

You cannot make any more sunlight.

You cannot make the sun set or rise at a different time.

You cannot make any more time, but you can waste what you have.

You cannot find anyone who knows where the time goes.

You cannot stop some people from looking for what is wrong so they can fix it.

You cannot get a degree by reading these *You Cannots*, but you can get a better education.

You cannot be willing to settle for less unless you are willing to accept what you get.

You cannot put lipstick on hogs and make them look any better.

You cannot stop success from coming to those that are too busy to look for it.

You cannot stop education from being forever.

You cannot stop knowledge from giving power.

You cannot put a time limit on how long education will last.

You cannot have enough supply of ability to satisfy the demand.

You cannot find any differences in a New York minute and any other minute.

You cannot measure break-neck speed.

You cannot find anyone who has seen greased lightning.

You cannot find anyone who has seen it rain cats and dogs.

You cannot stop God from knowing what is going on and what you are doing.

You cannot stop your life from having ups and downs if you sit next to the aisle in churches, theaters, or other meetings.

You cannot prevent the pen from being more powerful than the sword.

You cannot stop students from getting *D's* and *F's* if they have too many *Zees.*

You cannot lose weight if you get too much elbow exercise.

You cannot lie, cheat and steal, and not be hurt in the end.

You cannot fail to take some risks if you want to succeed.

You cannot stop wise men from creating more opportunities than they find.

You cannot depend on your eyes when your brain is not in gear.

You cannot find a more powerful planet than the sun.

You cannot refuse to go to your own funeral.

You cannot stop what is in the well from coming up in the bucket.

You cannot stop successful people from improving on other people's ideas to make them more successful.

You cannot stop some people from being as good as dead.

You cannot buy patience at a department store.

You cannot stop time from moving on.

You cannot prevent your children from getting Alzheimer's when they tell you they will call you back or do something that they said they would do and did not do it.

You cannot determine when or where your next itch will occur, but you can determine when and where to scratch.

You cannot stop knowledgeable people from gaining more knowledge.

You cannot have greater wisdom than to know what you do not know.

You cannot decrease crime by increasing leniency.

You cannot prevent some people from criticizing or complaining about someone else's work or original idea that they did not contribute anything to.

You cannot stop some people who were fishermen from becoming aquarium keepers.

You cannot depend on living with one person the rest of your life, except for yourself.

You cannot predict the future near as well as you can if you invent it.

You cannot stop a lot of people from giving instructions after they die through their will or trust.

You cannot be average unless you want to be the best of the worst or the worst of the best.

You cannot stop profanity from being a way that weak people try to show they are strong.

You cannot prevent becoming a stiff after you die.

You cannot make a splash if you go with the flow.

You cannot prevent traffic from bottling up when a soda truck stalls out.

You cannot prevent yourself from being the architect of your fortune.

You cannot need a vacation unless you have just had one.

You cannot get people to wait very long before scratching an itch.

You cannot get anything clean unless you get something else dirty.

You cannot prevent couch disease from causing your chest to fall into your belly.

You cannot get a much more satisfying feeling than to scratch an itch.

You cannot prevent schoolteachers from touching the future.

You cannot stop people from making lemonade and furniture polish from lemons.

You cannot call it work if it is something that you really want to get done to make you happy.

You cannot get couch potatoes to peel potatoes.

You cannot stop some people from getting better and getting over it.

119

You cannot stop doing nothing from being hard because you never know when you are finished.

You cannot be walking on solid ground if you are walking on eggs and jello.

You cannot stop some people from doing the impossible, but the difficult takes a little longer.

You cannot stop small drops of rain from causing big floods.

You cannot prevent history from teaching us what not to do as well as what to do.

You cannot stop people from conforming to their environment and where they live.

You cannot get gain without pain.

You cannot have success unless you have successors.

You cannot reject receiving wisdom unless you want to take the consequences of not having it.

You cannot make any more air.

You cannot get more enjoyment or good feeling from your fingernails than when they scratch an itch.

You cannot get household tasks to be easier and quicker than when they are done by somebody else.

You cannot stop some people from giving you all they have, even if it is the measles.

You cannot stop what you think about most of the time being what you think about.

You cannot stop education from being the product of knowledge.

You cannot have to worry two days a week; one is yesterday and the other one is tomorrow.

You cannot find anything scarcer than hen's teeth.

You cannot make wisdom less valuable than knowledge.

You cannot prevent people who have wisdom from obtaining knowledge.

You cannot prevent people from eventually coming before their final judge.

You cannot stop light from shining.

You cannot stop God from continuing to give, and not send a bill.

You cannot stop living; it will be in heaven or hell and it's your choice.

You cannot take God out of good and have anything left but 'o'.

You cannot stop yesterday from being history and today from being considered a gift. That is why we consider today as being *the present*.

You cannot stop time from escaping.

You cannot stop some people from doing what is right even when someone else is doing them wrong.

You cannot stop some people from saying they are under the weather, but you cannot find people that say they are over the weather.

You cannot stop *honest* disagreement from often being a good sign of progress.

You cannot stop some pain from being a good warning signal.

You cannot stop some pain from being the cause of great happiness.

You cannot use up the Sun's energy; it has a never-ending supply.

You cannot make a mountain out of a molehill.

You cannot stop three nails and one cross from adding up to '*4-giveness*'.

You cannot prevent today from being the first day of the rest of your life.

You cannot get anyone else except God to answer prayer.

You cannot increase your lifetime by smoking.

You cannot determine that there was a need for engineers to design and build Noah's Ark, but you can determine there was a need for better engineers to design and build the Titanic.

You cannot stop sitting in an easy chair from being real easy, but it is hard to get out of it.

You cannot lower your golf score by playing with slick golf grips.

You cannot have a greater fall than falling on your knees.

You cannot calm your temper by losing it.

You cannot stop some people from loving on back streets and living on Main Street.

You cannot stop dogs from thinking fire plugs are for their own personal use.

You cannot have a good kiss without a hug.

You cannot be good to children if you fail to give them discipline, not abuse, but discipline. The lack of discipline could cause them great harm.

You cannot stop a lot of collect phone calls from being placed on Mother's and Father's Day from being the days that the most collect phone calls are recorded.

You cannot get your teeth to be true to you when they are false.

You cannot stop most people from having three tongues; one in their mouth and two in their shoes.

You cannot stop some people from being dim wits even if you doubled the size of their brains.

You cannot stop the girls from getting prettier at closing time.

You cannot stop paying for ignorance and receiving rewards for knowledge.

You cannot earn unless you learn.

You cannot assume that couch potatoes eat a lot of potatoes.

You cannot prevent wisdom from being applied knowledge.

You cannot stop some golfers from throwing their clubs in the lake.

You cannot make things right if you do not know what is wrong.

You cannot prevent some people from thinking wisdom teeth give them wisdom.

You cannot stop babies from needing a lot of changes.

You cannot stop giving yourself experience.

You cannot prevent some people from graduating from obnoxious schools or universities.

You cannot find many people who are six feet above criticism.

You cannot stop some people from being kind, polite and sweet-spirited until you try to sit in their church pews.

You cannot nurse a grudge and make it get better.

You cannot stop doughnuts from surrounding their holes.

You cannot stop people from wanting to serve God, but only as advisors.

You cannot stop some people's minds from being like concrete, thoroughly mixed up, but permanently set.

You cannot prevent knowledge from speaking, but wisdom listens.

You cannot stop rainy days from being fare weather for cab drivers.

You cannot destroy your character by practicing integrity.

You cannot buy lasting peace with the devil.

You cannot stop some people's intelligence from being as shallow as a saucer.

You cannot prevent golf from being a game of controlled or mistake management.

You cannot get your best friend to turn against you if he is your dog.

You cannot stop lazy people from getting their rest before they get tired.

You cannot find a right way to go wrong.

You cannot get dizzy doing good turns.

You cannot convince some people from thinking their wants are necessities.

You cannot learn very much from the second kick of a mule.

You cannot stop seven days without prayer from making one weak.

You cannot have a more inexpensive way of improving your looks than a smile.

You cannot see your friends in hell because it is dark there.

You cannot stop God from being the good, bad and only weather maker.

You cannot be considered successful unless you leave this earth better than you found it.

You cannot prevent education (not degrees) from being the reason you make sufficient amounts of money to support you and your family well.

You cannot stop character from being what you are when no one else is looking.

You cannot stop some people from being like rose stems; if you fool with them, you will get stuck.

You cannot prevent people from already knowing a lot of these <u>You Cannots</u>, but this book is a good reminder.

You cannot destroy true love.

You cannot be fully dressed unless you are wearing a smile.

You cannot have a fire without air.

You cannot stop some people from having a lot of useless knowledge.

You cannot make lemons out of lemonade.

You cannot be expected to do anything in life except what is right.

You cannot be very dependable if you are always late for where you are supposed to be.

You cannot find a better four-letter word than love.

You cannot stop golf from being a fun-loving four-letter word.

You cannot get any answers when you talk to sheep; you should talk to the shepherd.

You cannot get golfers that hit the ball in the fairway to think the fairway is always fair.

You cannot prevent shoes from having soles; but they are much different from your own personal soul.

You cannot stop a lot of people from trusting in Christ to save them from going to hell.

You cannot get people who participate in spelling bees to swarm or sting.

You cannot make a tree; it takes a higher power.

You cannot stop some people from having once in a lifetime memories only once.

You cannot stop golfers from digging fishing worms.

You cannot have a lonely heart without looking sad.

You cannot prevent bad photos from making good memories.

You cannot prevent some young people from looking at old people and seeing a treasure.

You cannot stand taller than to be willing to stand corrected.

You cannot prevent obstacles from being another form of opportunities.

You cannot undo the past, but you can learn from it.

You cannot have a happy heart and your face not show it.

You cannot stop golf from causing you to have to think.

You cannot ruin the truth anymore than stretching it.

You cannot have the wind knocked out of your sail and easily stay on course.

You cannot get many people to wash a rental car.

You cannot be very successful unless you have a good education, and not just a degree.

You cannot read these *You Cannots* without improving your education.

You cannot have anything unless you have God's help.

You cannot run and hide from God.

You cannot prevent eating fruit from causing many jams.

You cannot un-ring a bell.

You cannot stop golf from being a fun-loving four letter word that makes you think of other four letter words: sand trap, hole, game, stop, roll back, sigh, hook, grip, putt, nine iron, card, fast, plug, hood, ball, path, shot, bank, heel, club, lake, good, and flag.

You cannot prevent other four letter words from being used on golf courses that are not used in church.

You cannot get trouble to take a holiday.

You cannot get some people to clean anything except their plates.

You cannot act like a skunk and not have someone notice.

You cannot stop piano tuners from eating tuna fish.

You cannot stop some people from when they are at their wit's end from finding God.

You cannot start peace much easier than starting with a smile.

You cannot stop some people from wanting to serve God, but only as an advisor.

You cannot get two wrongs to make a right.

You cannot find anything good about mosquitoes.

You cannot expect to get a better pastor unless you pray for the one you have.

You cannot stop the author of these *You Cannots* from repeating himself more than once.

You cannot destroy God's love.

You cannot stop some people from being polite and sweet-spirited until you try to sit in their church pews.

You cannot find straight bananas.

You cannot have a better vitamin for a Christian than B1.

You cannot allow your children to rule the house unless you want the environment to become unbearable.

You cannot bend or stretch the truth.

You cannot stop *'and in conclusion'* from being the best part of a speech.

You cannot live to be 100, unless you give up all the things that make you want to live to be 100.

You cannot see stars unless you look up at the sky.

You cannot find a perfect spouse; just think what they have to put up with and be thankful for what you have.

You cannot prevent some people from acting like they were baptized in persimmon juice.

You cannot grow old friends fast.

You cannot follow your dreams unless you wake up.

You cannot stop roses from having thorns that get your attention.

You cannot prevent any place from being within walking distance if you have the time.

You cannot prevent what is in the well from coming up in the bucket.

129

You cannot get a mirror to lie; it shows just what it sees.

You cannot find instant coffee instantly in a grocery store.

You cannot prevent the weather from having an effect on the size of the crowd that attends your funeral, no matter how much fame or fortune you may have.

You cannot stop God from giving.

You cannot stop lazy people from trying to find an easier, faster way of getting the job done.

You cannot get much benefit from a sun dial that is placed in the shade.

You cannot throw dirt and not lose ground.

You cannot grip a soap bubble.

You cannot get the red, white, and blue to run.

You cannot stop parents from getting smarter as their children grow older.

You cannot prevent God from knowing where you are at all times.

You cannot stop the parts of the body that cannot be seen from being the most important parts.

You cannot find anyone who is exactly like you.

You cannot prevent an ounce of prevention from being worth a pound of cure.

You cannot stop success from building more success.

You cannot find anyone who has seen greased lighting.

You cannot almost be saved without being totally lost.

You cannot find a substitute for honesty and truth.

You cannot find doing what is right to be wrong.

You cannot have arms long enough to box with God.

You cannot pick your parents.

You cannot find athletes who can spit nearly as often or as good as baseball players.

You cannot fail to get a prenuptial agreement signed before you get married if you want the prenuptial to be effective.

You cannot stop smoking from being a big cause of death.

You cannot buy yourself into heaven.

You cannot buy yourself out of hell.

You cannot control the height of waves in the oceans.

You cannot get by anything with the skin of your teeth.

You cannot control rainstorms, snowstorms, windstorms, ice storms, sleet storms, or any other form of nature.

You cannot spread happiness around without getting some of it on you.

You cannot stop libraries from disappearing when old people die.

You cannot stop propaganda from being the art of persuading others of what you don't believe.

You cannot stop bakeries from *doughnating* to good causes.

You cannot stop people who visit libraries from learning.

You cannot stop people from learning who read the Bible and dictionaries.

You cannot believe in love at first sight unless you take a second look.

You cannot stop the mice from playing when the cat is away.

You cannot have anything happen to you better than getting old.

You cannot stop diamonds from being a girl's best friend.

You cannot find anyone who has gotten blood out of a turnip.

You cannot beat an idea whose time has come.

You cannot stop golf courses from getting longer when you really get older.

You cannot find anyone who knows you any better than you know yourself.

You cannot stop up your ears with your fingers and hear some of the things you need to hear.

You cannot find people who are too lazy to not eat.

You cannot stop words from making people feel bad and good.

You cannot find paths that lead somewhere that do not have obstacles.

You cannot stop truth from always being in demand.

You cannot live a long life without reaching old age.

You cannot wait too long to accept Jesus Christ as your savior unless you want to go to hell instead of heaven.

You cannot prevent the honeymoon from being the time between bells and bills.

You cannot make volunteers worthless; they are priceless.

You cannot be too hard on your parents; if it were not for them, you would not be here.

You cannot find a self-made man.

You cannot find anyone who has blue blood.

You cannot stop students from bringing crab apples to mean, insulting teachers.

You cannot prevent most overweight people from continuing to overeat to keep being overweight.

You cannot stop golfers who hit the green more often from getting more '*green*'.

You cannot steal and not be guilty.

You cannot prevent toilet paper from being like life; the closer you get to the end, the faster it goes.

You cannot prevent experience from being a way of correcting your mistakes.

You cannot stretch the truth and not take the chance of it snapping back.

You cannot hide light.

You cannot get any benefits from unused knowledge.

You cannot stop reading from being the foundation of wisdom.

You cannot stop improving old ideas.

You cannot stop old people from spending a lot of time getting that way.

You cannot stop life from being like an escalator; you're either going up or down.

You cannot prevent the death rate from being the same everywhere in the world; one per person.

You cannot buy happiness if you don't know where to shop.

You cannot find anyone to sign the death warrant to your dreams except yourself.

You cannot stop God from giving birds their food, but he does not throw it in their nest.

You cannot stop an outhouse from being a house of great relief.

You cannot stop *'okey dokey'* from meaning okay.

You cannot measure pleasure.

You cannot stop some people's dictionary and Bible from always looking new because they never read them.

You cannot go to hell if you just do what is right.

You cannot get smokers from placing little value on their lives and the problems it causes others.

You cannot find anyone that can lick their elbow.

You cannot stop sailboats from always needing wind.

You cannot stay young if you live long enough.

You cannot teach your dog to swim because he already knows how.

You cannot have but one real God.

You cannot stop some people from being honored on April 1st of each year.

You cannot find many people who come to a complete stop at stop signs.

You cannot find anyone who has seen the straw that broke the camel's back.

You cannot be replaced if you are irreplaceable.

You cannot walk a mile in someone else's shoes without making your feet hurt.

You cannot test the depth of the water with both feet and be sure it won't cover your head.

You cannot have to remember what you said if you tell the truth.

You cannot lose some arguments if you just shut up.

You cannot stop thinkers from helping non-thinkers.

You cannot prevent thinkers from being in charge.

You cannot prevent fish from being the best upstream swimmers.

You cannot need to do any more in life than to just do what is right.

You cannot have anything to happen to you in life that is better than getting old.

135

You cannot succeed at sky diving if you are not successful the first time.

You cannot stop some people from wasting publicity regardless of whether it is good or bad.

You cannot stop a lot of young men from chasing women no more than you can stop a lot of old men from chasing golf balls.

You cannot stop some people that do not know their own mind from missing very much.

You cannot prevent getting old from being the greatest thing that could happen to you.

You cannot stop bachelors from being singled out at dance parties.

You cannot stop rocking chairs from moving you, but you don't get anywhere new.

You cannot have or pray a more perfect prayer than to say, "Dear Lord. Thank you for all of my many blessings. Amen."

You cannot be closer to your Mother than you were before you were born.

You cannot do wrong if you just do what is right. Do not delay.

You cannot stop some golfers from punishing their golf balls when they don't obey. They just throw them in the lake.

You cannot find anyone that has actually had the daylights scared out of them.

You cannot actually find anyone that has talked to a man in the moon.

You cannot ever stop building character.

You cannot stop a lot of golfers' handicaps from being woods and irons.

You cannot find some birds that don't stand up while they sleep.

You cannot expect your children to have or use common sense if you fail to teach them.

You cannot determine the ability or size of the brain because of the size of the person.

You cannot stop some people from being courteous, nice, and polite until they get behind the steering wheel of an automobile.

You cannot look through clear glass and see yourself, but if you add silver to the glass, you see a person that you like very much.

You cannot stop a lot of things from happening under the sun.

You cannot stop men from saying they are the head of the house and women saying they are the neck and they turn the head.

You cannot stop some people from growing older without growing up.

You cannot stop some people from saying the moon is made from a chunk of cheese; even though there are no cows or goats on the moon.

You cannot get finished building character.

You cannot stop silence from being ever so golden as when you have nothing to say.

You cannot fit in a social circle if you are a square.

You cannot lie without feeling guilty.

You cannot smoke without getting addicted.

You cannot walk before you crawl.

You cannot get fish to swim on the top of water.

You cannot stop the truth from always being the truth.

You cannot find anything more complicated than the human brain.

You cannot walk without exercising.

You cannot play baseball without a bat and ball.

You cannot determine that the author has used correct English in writing these *You Cannots*.

You cannot determine that a cucumber is any cooler than a tomato.

You cannot find any food that tastes good if you have lost your taste buds.

You cannot stop golfers for not believing that fairways are always fair.

You cannot stop people that have cold feet from having a warm heart.

You cannot find any place in the Bible that contradicts itself.

You cannot find anything more beautiful than a pretty woman.

You cannot find a tougher 'ritis man than author.

You cannot stop people from forgetting what '*what's his name's*' real name is.

You cannot find a more lethal weapon than the mouth.

You cannot daydream and watch your step at the same time.

You cannot keep some teenagers from cleaning up their room weakly.

You cannot prevent the author from continuing to write more <u>You Cannots</u>.

You cannot find it hard to forgive when the fault is yours.

You cannot underestimate the power of stupidity or education.

You cannot stop caterpillars from becoming butterflies.

You cannot stop some people from having unused space in their brain.

You cannot stop the cost of admission to heaven or hell from being zero, so don't delay in making up your mind where you want to go.

You cannot prevent a fender bender from making you feel like a wreck.

You cannot find anyone that knows how fast 'break neck speed' is or how fast 'greased lightening is.'

You cannot go to hell if you accept Jesus Christ as your savior and live by his word.

Yu cannot stop women from looking more classy in high heels that they do in flip-flops.

You cannot stop this book from giving the answers to a lot of people's problems and questions.

You cannot prevent all people, including all students, from needing one of these books; because they are educational, factual, fun, and true to life.

You cannot stop some people from having degrees while others have education.

You cannot stretch truth too far. It is like a rubber band and it will snap back and sting you.

You cannot notice housework that is done unless it is not done.

You cannot be doing too well in school if your teacher is glad when you miss a day.

You cannot stop some people's favorite vegetable from being carrot cake.

You cannot stop television from entertaining you with people that you would not allow in your home.

You cannot be envious of what other people have and increase what you have.

You cannot lie and have anything else to lose.

You cannot retire from learning if you want to stay up to date.

You cannot stop the fruit from falling close to the tree.

You cannot stop laziness from helping you to be poor.

You cannot be impolite, impudent, sarcastic, and insulting; and make many new friends, gain respect, and keep the friends you may have.

You cannot prevent the *'haves'* from helping the *'have nots'*.

You cannot find a better way to control your weight than just eating half of what is on your plate.

You cannot tell a lie and not have a *'liability'*.

You cannot find better tools than your hands.

You cannot learn to ride a bicycle by reading a book.

You cannot stop a lot of people from being uneducated because it is too easy and education requires work.

You cannot stop good and evil from being in some people.

You cannot build a house if you start to try to build the roof first.

You cannot start too soon to teach children not to waste if they want to have a good, economical, and plentiful life.

You cannot make any more stars.

You cannot need to do anything else in life except to just do what is right.

You cannot make any more time; so use it wisely.

You cannot make any more moonlight.

You cannot prevent the necessities of life from being food, shelter, and clothing.

You cannot increase your life expectancy by smoking.

You cannot get the golf course fairway to always be fair when your ball ends up in a divot.

You cannot overeat and under exercise, and not end up being overweight.

You cannot stop one week with no food from making one weak.

You cannot leave any of your education at school and not cheat yourself.

You cannot continue to do wrong and not eventually get caught.

You cannot give your heart good exercise by running up hill and running down people.

You cannot stop school football players from needing to tackle their books after practice and games.

You cannot have a deadline on telling the truth.

You cannot stop some people from saying this is in 'my neck of the woods' even though most people's necks are far from any woods.

You cannot make any more time.

You cannot stop love from being one of the most powerful influences in the world.

You cannot find a substitute for the truth.

You cannot stop some people from saying, "they can't" while others say, "they can."

About the Author

Roy L Matlock, Sr., now 83 years old, is living proof that you cannot stop an entrepreneur that just *'keeps on keeping on'*. Even though his family was very poor, they taught him right from wrong, to always show respect for others, and to work and make an honest living.

Mr. Matlock is a member of Judson Baptist church in Nashville, a 32nd degree Scottish Rite Mason, a Shriner, and a member of Richland Country Club. He has been married for 64 years.

He started his first business as a young boy picking up old paint cans at the city dump, boiling them out with lye water in a wash kettle, cleaning them, and selling them to paint stores for ten cents each. He later had three paper routes, which would ultimately lead him into a life of hard work and success.

As an industrious young man, he had a hard time holding a job because he was always trying to tell the boss what to do. The bosses did not like this and he got fired from his jobs. At age 20, he decided he had been fired for the last time and, thus, started a small welding shop of his own. He went door-to-door to businesses asking if they had anything broken that needed welding. This one-man shop, fueled by his work ethics and common sense philosophy, grew into a premiere Nashville-based truck body and semi-trailer manufacturing company of over 500 employees.

While in the business of manufacturing truck bodies and semi-trailers, and selling them throughout the US and Canada, he established a leasing, financing, and insurance agency to finance, lease, and insure the financing and leasing operations. He was also a truck manufacturer's dealer to sell, lease, and finance the equipment manufactured.

He sold his company in 1983. After his company was sold, he found that playing golf every day was not fully satisfying and was compelled to start another business building fully equipped, double drive-thru restaurants.

He is a man that knows how to design and build a wide variety of products, and one of his patented inventions is a unique Golf Grip Washer that makes golf grips feel new, tacky, and clean.

He has designed and copyrighted unique design extruded aluminum side panels that lock together the truck body, trailer, and portable storage unit that does not require thousands and thousands of rivets. He is now looking for someone, or a company, to manufacture and market this new design. He says if he were 25 years younger, he would start another company to manufacture and market these new products. For a free information package, you may contact him at his address herein.

Throughout his adult life, he continually generated common sense, educational, factual, fun and entertaining 'one-liners' beginning with "*You cannot* ..." His more than four thousand *You Cannots* are now presented in two volumes titled *You Cannots by Daddy Roy L. Matlock, Sr.* Among his favorite *You Cannots* are:

You Cannot recognize most opportunities because they are disguised as hard work.

You Cannot stop people from spending their money before they get it.

You Cannot find harder work than thinking ... that is why so many people don't do it.

You Cannot become financially independent unless you learn how to make money while you sleep.

You Cannot be denied success if you are a go-getter.

You Cannot get golf balls to listen when you talk to them … they turn off their hearing aids.

You Cannot prevent someone who teases their hair from looking irritated.

You Cannot stop some people from being honored on April 1st of each year.

At 83, Roy L. Matlock, Sr. still plays golf two days a week and, at the age of 82, he shot his age. His entrepreneurial spirit is still alive and well; and five days a week you can find him at his kitchen table, glasses on, and a yellow legal pad in hand, quickly writing down the many ideas that still pour freely from his mind; and continually writing *You Cannots*. He is living proof that *You Cannot* stop a vigorous entrepreneurial spirit that just '*keeps on keeping on*'.

Special Notice from the Author

I hope you have enjoyed reading my book of *You Cannots.* I have tried to make them fun, educational, factual, and true to life.

If you have enjoyed these *You Cannots* as much as I have enjoyed writing them, tell your friends, family, and neighbors so that they might get one of the books to read and have fun. I think all students should read this book to further their 'common sense' education.

Printed in the United States
77933LV00001B/118-216

9 781933 912547